Poetic Philosophy Presents

Narrative Translations Designed for Accessibility

Plato's Cratylus:
By Zeus!
A Tragic-Comedy About
the Possibility of a Common-Field of Truth

By Plato

Translated by Jason Kassel, PhD

© 2025

Recursive Publishing

Table of Contents

Introduction

Translating Cratylus as a Field of Shared Truth

I. Conceptual Fidelity Over Lineal Literalism

This translation of *Cratylus* differs in a crucial way from the well-known renderings by Benjamin Jowett and Harold N. Fowler. Their versions follow a relatively strict, line-for-line method, prioritizing word-for-word fidelity and closely mirroring the Greek phrase order, even at the cost of flattening Plato's dramatic metaphors. That is a valid and valuable tradition, preserving the skeleton of the argument in highly literal English.

My approach, by contrast, aims for conceptual fidelity. It preserves the exact sequence of Plato's reasoning — carefully aligned with the Stephanus pagination — while also drawing forward what is implicit in Plato's imagery, analogies, and dramatic framing. In the Greek, much of Plato's civic and mythic texture remains only half-spoken, relying on the cultural literacy of an Athenian audience. A modern reader risks missing that deeper orchestration unless it is surfaced through metaphor-sensitive translation.

II. Preserving Plato's Metaphoric Language

This version carries Plato's military metaphors — the hoplite phalanx, the shield and spear of logos — directly into the surface of the English. Where Plato gestures toward civic language as a Ship of Logos, this translation gives the metaphor fuller voice. These images are not decorative: they enact Plato's core concern with the integrity of shared reasoning, staged like a battle line in defense of truth.

A similar interpretive choice is made with the oath "By Zeus!" (μὰ τὸν Δία). Rather than render it loosely as an exclamation, I retain its original ritual form. Zeus was Zeus Horkios, the god of oaths, and his invocation in public speech functioned as a binding pledge — not casual rhetoric, but solemn accountability under divine witness. Plato repeats this phrase over a dozen times in *Cratylus*, often at moments of rhetorical turning. To modern ears, it may seem theatrical. But in Plato's context, it reinforces the gravity of speech as a civic and sacred act.

III. Logos and the Common Field of Truth

A further interpretive decision involves the word logos. Where Plato uses logos plainly — to mean "reason," "speech," or "argument" — I preserve it in that familiar sense. But in more philosophical passages, I have expanded its force to what I call the common-field of truth.

Plato's logos is never purely personal or private. In *Cratylus*, logos is a civic instrument, a public standard, and a battlefield — formed by a lawgiver, steered by a dialectician, and tested in shared struggle. Socrates does not ask whether words are correct in isolation, but whether they allow speakers to stand together in understanding. Thus, I render *logos* at times as common-field of truth: a deliberate phrase that makes visible Plato's deeper question — whether language can sustain a shared, stable space of meaning.

This phrase respects Plato's metaphors: the field is civic, cultivated, and defended. It is not imposed from above, but upheld through participation — what the Greeks called koinōnia (*sharing, communion*). This underlying concept, though not always named, is structurally central to *Cratylus*: the entire dialogue hinges on whether a koinōnia tou logou — a communion of reason — is possible.

IV. Koinōnia and the Stakes of Naming

This translation treats language not as technical designation, but as the medium of shared life. Plato's *Cratylus* tests whether names (ὀνόματα) can be correct by nature — not just by agreement or force. The dialogue contrasts slave-names (names imposed through domination) with names forged in accordance with nature and reason.

This is a fundamentally political and metaphysical question. If names are arbitrary, then the logos collapses, and no common reasoning remains. If they are rigidly natural but incommunicable, then we are left in solitary silence. Plato's answer lies in the middle: names must align with the nature of things, but they are made to serve a community — upheld through the koinōnia of dialectic, steered by reason toward shared truth.

This structure mirrors what Kant, centuries later, would call the communis sensus — a common sense that orients judgment toward universal validity, even when truth cannot be proven. Plato's *logos*, in this translation, becomes the ancestor of Kant's Gemeinsinn: not a private assertion, but a public offering — the disciplined act of entering a field where truth can be defended without domination.

V. A Translation Designed for Conceptual Integrity

In that spirit, this is not a line-for-line translation in the narrow sense, but a line-for-concept translation. Every philosophical idea appears in sequence; every pivot in argument is preserved. But the English is sculpted to carry forward the poetic, tragic, and civic textures that Plato's Greek would have conveyed to his audience.

My hope is that this method restores Plato's full voice — as philosopher, dramatist, and civic poet — for readers who might otherwise encounter only the logical skeleton of his reasoning. In doing so, this *Cratylus* translation seeks to preserve the most urgent question of all:

> Can we still stand together in a common field of truth?

That is Plato's question. It is also ours.

Glossary of Translation Choices

This glossary clarifies and defends the translation choices made throughout this edition. Where Plato's Greek is dense with metaphor, civic imagery, or ritual language, I have adopted renderings that preserve not only the surface meaning but also the deeper dramatic and cultural force. Terms like *slave-name*, *phalanx of logos*, and *common-field of truth* are explained here so that readers can see how they align with Plato's original Greek vocabulary and intention. This glossary ensures transparency and invites the reader to judge how these choices hold together Plato's vision of a shared, reasoned field of truth.

Common Field of Truth

- Greek basis: κοινὸν πεδίον ἀληθείας (conceptual, built from *κοινωνία* "sharing," *ἀληθής* "true," *πεδίον* "field")

- Reason: makes vivid Plato's repeated concern that truth must be defended in a shared social arena, echoing hoplite battlefields.

Slave-name

- Greek: δουλων ὀνόματα (δοῦλος = slave, ὄνομα = name)

- Reason: stresses that renaming is an exercise of raw domination, as in the aftermath of war, rather than a polite "servant" label.

Phalanx of Logos

- Greek: λογῶν φάλαγξ

- Reason: Plato likens correct speech to a disciplined battle line, coordinated in defense of reason.

Lord of the City

- Greek: ἄστυ + ἄναξ (Ἀστυάναξ)

- Reason: ties to Homeric images of the "city-lord" as protector and upholder of names, linking correct language to civic stability.

Machina

- Greek: μηχανή

- Reason: captures Plato's dramatic sense of a mechanism or a divine inspiration that moves argument forward, echoing tragic stage machinery.

By Zeus!

- Greek: μὰ τὸν Δία / ὦ Ζεῦ

- Reason: literal retention of a solemn oath marking rhetorical shifts, highlighting the divine witness to truth-claims.

Foreign / Barbarian

- Greek: βάρβαρος, ξένος

- Reason: preserves the political tension between Athenian identity and "other" cultures, central to

Plato's exploration of naming's universality.

Ship of Logos

- Greek imagery: κυβερνήτης (pilot), πλοῖον (ship), πηδάλιον (rudder)

- Reason: Plato's extended ship imagery frames the collective task of steering reasoning toward shared truth.

Spear of Logos

- Greek: λόγου δόρυ

- Reason: draws on Homeric epic weaponry, showing names as weapons that can strike truthfully or falsely.

Shield of Reason

- Greek: λογισμοῦ ἀσπίς

- Reason: following Plato's hoplite field metaphors, the shield protects the reasoning phalanx from error.

Sword of Confidence

- Greek: θάρρους ξίφος (Socrates' phrase of "standing firm")

- Reason: part of the martial metaphor set — courage as the inner blade that prevents collapse of shared argument.

Lawgiver / Name-maker

- Greek: νομοθέτης, ὀνοματοθέτης

- Reason: Plato's figure of the lawgiver is elevated to one who establishes correct names, upholding civic order.

Possession / Inspired Madness

- Greek: θεία μοῖρα, ἐνθουσιασμός

- Reason: Socrates describes a spirit overtaking him, a "possession" that fuels the argument like tragic frenzy.

Astyanax ("Lord of the City")

- Greek: Ἀστυάναξ

- Reason: carefully retained because Plato links correct naming to preserving civic truth, with the wise men of Troy naming Hector's son as protector.

Dialectician as Pilot

- Greek: κυβερνήτης τοῦ λόγου

- Reason: emphasizes Plato's distinction that the dialectician alone can steer speech rightly, supervising even the lawgiver.

Shipwright of Logos

- Greek: ναυπηγός τοῦ λόγου

- Reason: mirrors Plato's use of artisanship — the shipwright's craft is analogous to crafting correct names.

Eternal / Unchanging

- Greek: ἀΐδιον, ἀκίνητον

- Reason: preserves Plato's exploration of whether names can hold fixed truth, contrasting with flux.

Divine Name

- Greek: θεῖον ὄνομα

- Reason: Socrates distinguishes human naming from "the names the gods themselves use," marking divine language as a standard beyond human convention.

Common Reason / Shared Reason

- Greek: κοινωνία τοῦ λόγου

- Reason: captures the idea that correct naming is a *civic* rather than private act, sustaining a communal reason.

Prologos

383a-383a: Cratylus' Resignation

Hermogenes: Cratylus, Socrates has arrived. Shall we — three old hoplites, defenders of the city — marshal our skills in speech? Let each man carry his *spear of logos* to pierce through confusion, and hold his *shield of reason* to keep the field. Let him also bear his *sword of confidence*, so that if our line should break, he can still stand firm. Together, we can form a *phalanx of logos*, sharing our reasoning to build a *common field of truth*. Shall we test whether a truly shared understanding of speech and thought can be forged?

Cratylus: If you think that is best.

383a-384a: Hermogenes Outlines Cratylus' Position

Hermogenes: Socrates, let me explain why I have brought this up. Our friend Cratylus argues that names are not merely conventions agreed upon by people, but that each name has a natural correctness. He says there is a truth in names that applies equally to Greeks and to barbarians — names are not simply sounds we attach to things by custom, but possess an inherent rightness.

So I asked him, "Is your own name truly 'Cratylus'?" and he answered yes. Then I asked about you, Socrates, and he again said yes. So I pressed him: "If that is so, wouldn't it follow that every person's name is the name by which they are called?" But he insisted, "Not for you — if everyone in the world called you Hermogenes, that still would not be your true name."

Since then, I have been trying to get a clearer answer from him, but he only replies with hints and riddles. He acts as if I am unfit to join his *phalanx of logos*, refusing to share reason, behaving as though he has some private insight he will not reveal — yet implying that if he did explain it fully, I would be completely convinced.

In this way, we cannot engage in shared reasoning, and he has blocked the possibility of a *common field of truth*.

So, Socrates, could you help interpret what Cratylus's mysterious oracle really means? Or better still, through shared reason, would you tell me what you yourself think about the correctness or truth of names? I would far rather hear your view.

384a-384c: Socrates Questions Hermogenes' Name

Socrates: Hermogenes, son of Hipponicus, there is an old saying that knowledge of what is truly good is hard to gain, and knowledge of names is no small part of that challenge. If I had been able to afford Prodicus's famous fifty-drachma course — which, as he himself claims, provides a complete education in language and grammar — I would already have the knowledge needed to answer you straightaway about the correctness of names. But in fact I only ever heard the single-drachma version, and so I cannot claim to know the full truth of these matters.

However, I am ready to stand beside you and Cratylus, to join our ranks in a *phalanx of logos*, and go together in search of what is correct, holding our shields of reason shoulder to shoulder, so that we may build a *common field of truth*.

As for what Cratylus says about your name — that "Hermogenes" is not truly your name — I suspect he is teasing you, perhaps implying that you do not live up to your namesake, Hermes, since you are always chasing after fortune and luck, but fail to catch them.

Still, as I said, this is difficult terrain to cross. Naming, like all knowledge of high matters, is hard to master. So let us join our reasoning, keep our line unbroken, and test whether you are right or Cratylus is right, until together we can reach firm ground upon our *common field of truth*.

384c-384e: Hermogenes and Slave-Names

Hermogenes: For my part, Socrates, I have often spoken about this with Cratylus and with many others, and I cannot convince myself that there is any principle of correctness in names beyond convention and agreement. It seems to me that whatever name you assign to a thing is its name, and if you give up that name and replace it with another, then the new name is just as correct as the old.

It is just as we do with those human beings who are subjugated and chained after war, granted their lives in exchange for bondage: we change their given names to *slave-names*, and in practice this new name is no less useful or serviceable than the one before. I believe that no name belongs to anything by nature; rather, its usage is fixed by the habit and custom of those who employ it.

But if this is not correct, then I am willing to listen and to learn, whether from Cratylus or from anyone else who can help steady our line of reason and bring us to a *common field of truth*.

385a-385c: Preparing the Field for Shared Reason

Socrates: You may well be right, Hermogenes. But let us examine this together. Your argument is that the name of each thing rests on convention and agreement — that it is simply whatever people agree to call it, no different from assigning *slave names* to those who are subjugated and chained after war?

Hermogenes: Yes, that is what I think.

Socrates: And this would hold true whether the *slave name* is given by an individual or by the state?

Hermogenes: Yes, exactly.

Socrates: Very well, then, let me put this to the test. Suppose I assign a *slave name* to something — for example, calling what we now call a "hoplite" a "warhorse," and what we now call a "warhorse" a "hoplite." Would the true name of the thing be "hoplite" for the public and "warhorse" for me alone, or the reverse — "warhorse" for the public and "hoplite" for me alone? Is that what you mean? And tell me — would such a practice truly create the possibility of *shared reason*, after we have formed a *phalanx of logos* to stand together?

Hermogenes: Yes, that is my opinion.

Socrates: Hermogenes, let me ask you this. In your view, is there such a thing as speaking the truth and speaking falsehood?

Hermogenes: Yes, there is.

Socrates: Then speech can be true or false?

Hermogenes: Certainly.

Socrates: And true speech would be speech that describes things as they truly are, while false speech would describe things as they are not?

Hermogenes: Yes.

Socrates: So speech allows us to say what is — and also what is not?

Hermogenes: Of course.

Socrates: Tell me, then: can true speech be true as a whole if its parts are untrue?

Hermogenes: No — its parts must also be true.

Socrates: Every part, or only the larger ones?

Hermogenes: Every part, I would say.

Socrates: Within speech, is there anything smaller than a name?

Hermogenes: No — the name is the smallest unit.

Socrates: And a name is spoken as part of true speech?

Hermogenes: Yes.

Socrates: Then, as you just agreed — if we hold our reasoning together about names, it becomes possible to establish shared reason and build a common field of truth.

Hermogenes: Yes, that follows.

385c-386a: Rejecting Protagoras

Socrates: And a part of false speech must also be false, correct?

Hermogenes: It must.

Socrates: Then you agree it is possible to utter either a false name or a true name, just as speech itself may be true or false? If that is so, then the name — the *spear of logos* — can strike truly or falsely within a sentence only if its smallest spear-tip remains strong. Otherwise, the *phalanx of logos* could never hold the field in defense of reason.

Hermogenes: Yes, that follows.

Socrates: So then, according to your view, the name for a person or thing is whatever each person says?

Hermogenes: Yes.

Socrates: It is possible for there to be as many names for each thing as everyone chooses to say? At the moment they speak, a name could be a true name?

Hermogenes: Yes, Socrates. I cannot see any other principle of correctness in names than this: I might assign something a slave name, and you might assign it your own slave name. That is what I observe. Cities and nations each impose their own names on things. Greeks differ from other Greeks in their slave names, and Greeks differ from barbarians in their naming as well.

Socrates: Now, Hermogenes, let us examine this. Do you think that reality is truly separate for each person — as Protagoras claimed, with his doctrine that "man is the measure of all things?" Do you truly believe things are for me as they seem to me, and for you as they seem to you? Or, do you think that things have some fixed and stable reality of their own?

Hermogenes: Socrates, I have sometimes found myself so perplexed that I have been *carried away*, as if possessed by Protagoras' spirit, drawn into his doctrine against my better judgment. It was like being seized by a daimon that confused my reason and pulled me out of my own place. But I do not truly believe he is correct.

386a-387b: By the Gods! (Good and Bad Men)

Socrates: And tell me — have you ever been carried away so completely that you ceased to believe there are any wicked men at all?

Hermogenes: By the gods, no! If anything, I have been carried away far more often by a contrary force, convinced — even overwhelmed — that there are certain men, and not a few of them, who are truly very bad.

Socrates: And have you never thought there were men who were very good?

Hermogenes: Very few, Socrates.

Socrates: But you did think there were at least some?

Hermogenes: Yes.

Socrates: And what is your opinion about them? Are the truly good men also truly wise, and the truly bad men truly foolish?

Hermogenes: Yes, that is what I believe.

Socrates: Now if Protagoras is right — if it is true, as he claims, that things are to each person exactly as they seem to that person — could some of us be wise while others are foolish?

Hermogenes: No, that would not be possible.

Socrates: So you see, Hermogenes, if wisdom and folly truly exist, then Protagoras cannot be correct. For if whatever appears to each person is really true to that person, then no one could ever be wiser than anyone else, and no one could stand out as a champion within the *phalanx of logos*. We would lose all measure of shared reason, and there could be no common field of truth at all.

Hermogenes: Yes, Socrates, that is exactly right.

Socrates: I suppose you also disagree with Euthydemus, who claims that all things equally belong to all men, at all times and forever? Because in his view as well, there could be no difference between the good and the bad — if virtue and its opposite were always held equally by everyone.

Hermogenes: No, that cannot be true.

387b-388e: Naming as a Craft and Instrument

Socrates: So if neither of these positions is right — if things do not equally belong to all men all the time, and are not defined individually for each person — then it must be clear that things have a fixed reality of their own. They do not change back and forth with our fancies, nor are they determined merely by our shifting opinions. They stand in relation to their own nature, set by nature itself, beyond our private wishes or chance agreements.

Hermogenes: Yes, Socrates, that seems to me correct.

Socrates: And tell me — if things themselves possess such a fixed nature, should their actions be any different? Or are not actions also a real class of things?

Hermogenes: Certainly, actions are as real as things.

Socrates: Then actions, too, must be performed according to their own nature, not merely according to our opinions about them. For example, if we set out to cut something — such as wood for our shared *Ship-of-Logos* — should we cut however we please, with whatever instrument we please? Or, if we are to cut rightly, should we not use the proper instrument, and cut in accordance with the nature of cutting? Isn't it true that if we try to cut contrary to nature, we will achieve nothing and fail?

Hermogenes: I think it is exactly as you say, Socrates — only by following nature can the action succeed.

Socrates: Then, too, if we undertake to burn something — perhaps timber to bend it into shape for our *Ship-of-Logos* — we should not burn it in just any fashion according to random opinion, but in the right way, with the proper instrument, and according to the nature of burning and being burned?

Hermogenes: Yes, that is true.

Socrates: And would you agree this same principle holds for all other actions as well — that they must be guided by their own nature, and carried out with their proper instruments, if they are to succeed?

Hermogenes: Certainly, Socrates.

Socrates: And speaking, Hermogenes — that is also a kind of action, is it not?

Hermogenes: Yes, of course.

Socrates: Then tell me this: if a man speaks merely according to his own fancy, will he create a space for a *phalanx of logos* to build shared reason and the possibility of a common field of truth? Will he speak rightly? Or rather, will he only succeed in creating shared reason through speech if he uses the instrument of speech in the way that is natural for speaking — and in the way things are meant to be spoken? Otherwise, if he ignores that natural measure, will he not fail entirely, and break apart the *phalanx of logos*, destroying any hope of shared reason and the possibility of defending a common field of truth?

Hermogenes: Yes, Socrates, I completely agree.

Socrates: Now naming itself is a part of speaking, is it not? Since in naming, people utter speech.

Hermogenes: Yes, certainly.

Socrates: And if speaking is a kind of action, directed toward things, then naming, too, must be a kind of action?

Hermogenes: Yes, that follows.

Socrates: But we have agreed that actions are not just relative to us, but possess a separate nature of their own?

Hermogenes: That is true.

Socrates: Then naming, too, if we are to remain consistent with everything we have established, cannot be done simply at our own pleasure. We must use the instrument and the way which the nature of things prescribes. If we pursue that course, then naming will succeed, helping us defend our *phalanx of logos* and safeguard shared reason. But if we disregard the nature of naming, we will fail, and the common field of truth will collapse.

Hermogenes: I think you are exactly right, Socrates.

Socrates: And again, Hermogenes, when something must be cut — as we agreed — it must be cut with something, must it not?

Hermogenes: Certainly, Socrates.

Socrates: And what must be woven, must be woven with something; and what must be bored, must be bored with something?

Hermogenes: Of course.

Socrates: And in the same way, what must be named, must be named with something?

Hermogenes: Yes, that is true.

Socrates: So tell me — what is it we use to bore a plank for our *Ship-of-Logos*?

Hermogenes: A borer.

Socrates: And what do we use to weave the sail that will catch the winds of reason?

Hermogenes: A shuttle.

Socrates: And what do we use, then, to name, so that the ship may be steered rightly and its crew may share reason together?

Hermogenes: A name.

Socrates: Exactly. A name, then, is a kind of instrument — no different in principle than the borer or the shuttle

— and it must be fitted to its task if our *Ship-of-Logos* is to sail truly toward the common field of truth.

Hermogenes: I see it clearly, Socrates.

Socrates: Then if I were to ask you, Hermogenes, "What kind of instrument is a shuttle?" would you not answer that it is an instrument with which we weave?

Hermogenes: Yes, of course.

Socrates: And what do we do, precisely, when we weave? Do we not separate and organize the mingled threads of warp and woof, so they hold together?

Hermogenes: Yes, that is true.

Socrates: And you could give similar answers about the borer, and other tools we might use to build and fit the timbers of our *Ship-of-Logos*, could you not?

Hermogenes: Certainly, Socrates.

Socrates: Then suppose I asked you the same kind of question about a name. Since a name is an instrument, what do we do with it, when we name?

Hermogenes: I cannot tell.

Socrates: Do we not, through names, teach one another, and separate things according to their natures, so that we can build shared reason together?

Hermogenes: Yes, certainly.

Socrates: Then a name is an instrument of teaching, and of distinguishing reality, just as a shuttle is an instrument for separating and ordering the threads of a sail — so that our *Ship-of-Logos* may hold its course and find the common field of truth.

Hermogenes: That is clear, Socrates.

Socrates: And the shuttle, Hermogenes — that is the instrument of the weaver, is it not?

Hermogenes: Of course, Socrates.

Socrates: Then the weaver will use the shuttle well, and "well" means he will use it as a skilled weaver uses it. And the teacher, in turn, will use a name well, and "well" means he will use it as a teacher, guiding shared reason.

Hermogenes: Yes, that is true.

Socrates: Now, when the weaver uses the shuttle skillfully, whose work is he using well?

Hermogenes: That of the carpenter, who made it.

Socrates: And is every man a carpenter, or only the one who has the proper skill?

Hermogenes: Only the one who has the skill.

Socrates: And when someone uses a borer to fit the timbers of our *Ship-of-Logos*, whose work is he using?

Hermogenes: The smith's.

Socrates: And is every man a smith, or only the one who possesses that craft?

Hermogenes: Only the one with the skill.

Socrates:

And when the teacher uses a name, Hermogenes, whose work is he putting to use?

Hermogenes:

That, Socrates, I cannot say.

Socrates:

Can you not tell even this — who gives us the names that we use?

Hermogenes:

No, I truly cannot.

Socrates:

Do you not think it is the law that gives us those names, like a craftsman forging the tools for our *phalanx of logos*?

Hermogenes:

That is very likely, Socrates.

388e-390b: Introducing the Lawgiver

Socrates: Then the teacher, when he uses a name to guide shared reason, is using the work of a lawgiver?

Hermogenes: I think that is right.

Socrates: And is every man a lawgiver, or only the one who has the proper skill to lay down names that can hold firm, like rivets in the planks of our *Ship-of-Logos*?

Hermogenes: Only the one who has that skill, Socrates.

Socrates: Then, Hermogenes, only the lawgiver may truly be called a *name-maker*. Among all men, and among all artisans, he is the rarest.

Hermogenes: So it seems, Socrates.

Socrates: Then consider what the lawgiver has in view when he gives names. Look at it in light of what we have already said. Tell me — what does the carpenter have in view when he makes a shuttle for weaving the sails of our *Ship-of-Logos*? Is it not the nature of the shuttle, the thing whose purpose is to weave rightly?

Hermogenes: Certainly.

Socrates: And if the shuttle should break while he is making it, would he make another by copying the broken one? Or would he look instead to the true form — the pattern of what a shuttle properly is — according to which he was shaping the one that broke?

Hermogenes: To that true form, I should think.

Socrates: Then we might very properly call that true form the real, or ideal, shuttle — the pattern he holds in mind to guide his skill?

Hermogenes: Yes, Socrates, I think that is exactly right.

Socrates: Then, Hermogenes, whenever a craftsman has to make a shuttle — whether for weaving a light garment or a heavy one, linen or wool or any other cloth — each of those shuttles must still contain the form, the *ideal* of shuttle, must it not? And in each one he must embody the nature that is best suited for that weaving?

Hermogenes: Yes, certainly.

Socrates: And the same principle applies to all other tools. The skilled artisan must discover the instrument naturally fitted to each purpose, and then he must shape that instrument in the proper material — not according to his own random will, but according to the nature of the task. For example, he must know how to shape in iron the borer properly suited by nature to drill the timbers of our *Ship-of-Logos*.

Hermogenes: Certainly, Socrates.

Socrates: And he must know how to shape in wood the shuttle best suited by nature for each kind of weaving, so the sail of our ship may hold firm in the winds of reason.

Hermogenes: That is true.

Socrates: For each kind of shuttle, it seems, is fitted by nature to its particular kind of weaving — and the same principle holds for all other instruments.

Hermogenes: Yes, Socrates.

Socrates: Then, my dear friend, must not the lawgiver — who alone is rightly the name-maker — also know how to embody, within sounds and syllables, that name which is fitted by nature for each thing? Must he not give all names with his eye fixed on the *ideal* name, if he is to be a true lawgiver and guide for our *phalanx of logos*? And even if different lawgivers do not embody that form in the same syllables, we should not forget the ideal name for that reason. For it enables shared reason and the possibility of a common field of truth.

Consider that different smiths, though they may be making the same tool for the same purpose, do not all cast their iron in exactly the same way; yet so long as they preserve the same ideal pattern, the tool is still true to its purpose, whether made here or among foreigners — is that not so?

Hermogenes: Certainly, Socrates.

Socrates: Then, on this basis, you will judge the lawgiver — whether he stands among our own city or rules in a foreign land — by whether he gives each thing its proper form of name through the right syllables. For so long as he fixes names according to their nature, he secures the possibility of shared reason and the defense of a common field of truth, wherever he may work.

Hermogenes: Certainly, Socrates.

390b-390d: Introducing the Dialectician

Socrates: Then tell me, Hermogenes, who is more likely to know whether the proper form of a shuttle has been embodied in any piece of wood: the carpenter who made it, or the weaver who must use it?

Hermogenes: I would say the one who is to use it, Socrates.

Socrates: And who uses the work of the lyre-maker? Surely the man who knows how to direct the making of the lyre and judge whether it is well made or not?

Hermogenes: Yes, certainly.

Socrates: And who is that?

Hermogenes: The lyre-player.

Socrates: And who will best judge the shipwright's work in building the Ship-of-Logos?

Hermogenes: The pilot.

Socrates: Then who, Hermogenes, is best suited to establish the phalanx of logos and guide the work of the lawgiver — the one who lays down names? Who can best judge whether those names are truly fixed to the nature of things, whether here or in a foreign land, so that they secure the possibility of a common field of truth? According to what we have said, must it not be the user?

Hermogenes: Yes, of course.

Socrates: And isn't the user of names best suited when he handles them as tools — precisely because he knows how to ask questions and test answers? The one most suited, then, is the man who works always with the objective of forming shared reason, so that a common field of truth may stand defended?

Hermogenes: Certainly, Socrates.

Socrates: And this same person, who is best suited to use names rightly, must also know how to make replies for the same purpose, must he not?

Hermogenes: Yes.

Socrates: Then isn't 'dialectician' the name rightly attached to the one who uses these tools — who knows how to ask questions and give answers? Is it not the dialectician who ensures the phalanx of logos holds its line, so that shared reason may stand?

Hermogenes: Yes, that is what I would call him.

Socrates: The carpenter who makes a rudder to steer the Ship-of-Logos must do so under the direction of the pilot, if that rudder is truly to hold the ship's course.

Hermogenes: Evidently, Socrates.

Socrates: In the same way, does it not follow that the work of the lawgiver is to give names, and that if those names are to steer rightly, the dialectician must direct him — acting as the rudder of logos for the lawgiver?

Hermogenes: That is true.

390d-391b: Correcting a Rigid Hermogenes

Socrates: Then, Hermogenes, the giving of slave-names cannot be done in the casual way you once imagined. It cannot be a careless task, nor one left to random men. I agree with Cratylus: names belong to things by nature. Because of this, not every person is fit to craft them. Only the one who looks to the proper name, the name given by nature to each thing, is able to shape names according to their true form in letters and syllables. Only such a person can lay down even slave-names in a way that steadies the phalanx of logos and defends the possibility of a common field of truth.

Hermogenes: Socrates, I do not know how to answer you. I have not yet reached a place of shared reason. It is not easy for me to change my conviction so suddenly. I think you would be more likely to convince me — and allow me to stand in your phalanx of logos — if you showed me exactly what you mean by the natural correctness of names.

Socrates: My dear Hermogenes, I have nothing certain to show. You forget what I told you earlier — that I did not pay for Prodicus' fifty-drachma teaching. I do not know, but I am willing to stand beside you in forming a phalanx of logos to search for the truth. And through this searching together, you and I have already seen something we did not see before: that names do indeed possess a kind of natural correctness, and that not every person knows how to assign even slave-names to things. Is that not true?

Hermogenes: Yes, certainly.

391b-391d: Initiating a Phalanx of Logos

Socrates: Then, if you wish to know, our next task is to try to discover what kind of correctness properly belongs to names.

Hermogenes: I do wish to know, Socrates.

Socrates: Then reflect with me.

Hermogenes: How should I reflect?

Socrates: The best way to investigate, my friend, is to enlist the help of those who claim to know. You gain their favor by paying them money — the sophists, for example, from whom your brother Callias gained his reputation for wisdom by paying them handsomely. But since you do not control your inheritance, you should go to him and beg him, entreat him, to teach you what he learned from Protagoras about the correctness of names.

Hermogenes: That would be absurd, Socrates, if I — who reject Protagoras' book the *Truth* altogether — were to pretend to value anything that he claims.

Socrates: Then if you cannot follow Protagoras, you should learn instead from Homer and the other poets.

Hermogenes: What does Homer say about names, Socrates, and where does he say it?

Parados

391d-392e: Homer and the Correctness of Names

Socrates: In many passages, Hermogenes, Homer most splendidly — and terribly — marks the difference between the names given by gods and those given by men. Surely in those verses he gives us profound and fearsome lessons about the correctness of names. For the gods — whose sight pierces through all illusions — must name things in accordance with their true nature. Don't you agree?

Hermogenes: I would expect nothing less from the gods, Socrates. But what examples do you have in mind?

Socrates: Surely you remember, Hermogenes, the tale of Achilles' wrath upon the corpse-choked plain of Troy? How the river, swollen with the bodies of fallen warriors, rose in fury against blazing Hephaestus, striving to quench its own blood-flooded banks. Homer tells us that this river was known among the gods — who see through to its elemental being — as *Xanthus*. But men call it *Scamander*, for we wade through history's blood-muddied shallows and speak only from habit and custom.

Hermogenes: Yes, I remember that well, Socrates.

Socrates: Well then, Hermogenes, do you think it is a mere small thing to know that this river is rightly called *Xanthus* by the gods, rather than *Scamander* by men? Or would you consider what Homer says of the bird which the gods name *Chalcis*, but men call *Cymindis*. Isn't it far more fitting to call it *Chalcis* in accord with its true nature? How about the hill which men call *Batieia*? Homer tells us the gods call it *Myrina's tomb*? There are many such teachings in Homer and in other poets.

Yet perhaps these matters lie beyond the power of our human phalanx of logos to grasp fully, for they reach too high, even beyond the corpse-strewn fields of Troy. It is, I think, more within human measure to inquire into the names *Scamandrius* and *Astyanax* — for Homer says these belong to Hector's son. Perhaps in these, we may better test what sort of correctness Homer believed belonged to names. You remember, of course, the lines I mean?

Hermogenes: I do, Socrates.

Socrates: Then tell me, Hermogenes, which name do you think Homer judged more correct for Hector's son — *Astyanax* or *Scamandrius*?

Hermogenes: I cannot say, Socrates.

Socrates: Consider it this way. If someone asked you, "Who gives names with greater correctness, the wise or the unwise?" — how would you answer?

Hermogenes: I would say the wise, of course.

Socrates: And in a city, taken as a whole, are men generally wiser, or women?

Hermogenes: The men, I would say.

Socrates: Now you remember, Homer tells us that the men of Troy called the child *Astyanax*, the lord of the city, while the women called him *Scamandrius*.

Hermogenes: Yes, I recall that.

Socrates: And Homer surely believed the men of Troy were wiser than their wives?

Hermogenes: That seems clear.

Socrates: Then Homer must have judged *Astyanax* the more fitting name, one that fixed the child's nature more firmly in the field of truth, since the wise named him so.

Hermogenes: So it appears, Socrates.

Socrates: Hermogenes, if we wish to understand shared reason and preserve the possibility of a common field of truth, let us consider why Homer anchors his verse with the name *Astyanax*. Does he not signal the reason most powerfully when he declares, *"He alone defended their city and long walls"*?

It is fitting that the son of such a steadfast shield-bearer should be called *Lord of the City*. He stood firm in the phalanx of logos and steered the rudder of the ship of logos, defending what his father had guarded. In this way, Astyanax preserved the possibility of a common field of truth.

392e-393c: By Zeus! (Hermogenes Contradicts Himself)

Hermogenes: Yes, Socrates, that is clear to me now.

Socrates: Hermogenes, do you really? I do not yet fully grasp it myself. You understand?

Hermogenes: No, by Zeus! Socrates, I do not.

Socrates: But, my good friend, did not Homer himself also give Hector his name?

Hermogenes: Why do you ask that?

Socrates: Because it seems to me that the name *Hector* is closely related to *Astyanax*. Both are Greek, and both suggest rulership. For *anax* means lord, and *hektor* means holder, and surely the one who is lord of something is also its holder: he possesses it, rules it, and guards it. Or do you think I am speaking nonsense, imagining that I have found a clue to Homer's understanding of the correctness of names?

Hermogenes: No, by Zeus, Socrates — I think you are on the right track.

Socrates: It seems reasonable, doesn't it, to call a lion's offspring a lion, and a horse's offspring a horse? I am not speaking of monstrous or unnatural births — for example, if a horse were to bring forth a calf contrary to nature, we would call that creature a calf, not a colt. And if a human being produced something inhuman, it should not be called a human. The same applies to trees and all other living things. Would you agree?

Hermogenes: Yes, Socrates, I agree.

393c-394b: Socrates Advises Vigilance

Socrates: Good, Hermogenes — but stay vigilant, and do not let me slip a trick past you! By the same reasoning, then, the offspring of a king should be called a king. And whether the name is formed from one set of syllables or another makes no difference, so long as its meaning is preserved. Even the addition or subtraction of letters does not matter, provided the name still holds and expresses the essence of the thing, so that its true nature is made plain.

Hermogenes: What exactly do you mean, Socrates?

Socrates: Nothing too difficult. Think of how we name the letters of the alphabet. We do not simply speak the letters themselves, except for four — epsilon, upsilon, omicron, omega — but for the rest, we add other sounds to make their names. As long as the letter's force is made clear within the name, it is still properly named. Take the letter beta, for instance. We add eta, tau, and alpha to it, but this does no harm, because the whole name still reveals what the lawgiver meant to designate. That shows how precisely names can be given, even to letters.

Hermogenes: Yes, Socrates, I believe you are right.

Socrates: Does not the same logic apply to kings? A king's son will probably be a king, a good man's son good, a handsome man's son handsome, and so on — the offspring of each class should naturally belong to that same class, unless there is some monstrous or unnatural birth. So their names, too, should follow the same pattern. But, Hermogenes, there can still be differences in syllables, so that to the untrained ear names might seem different, even though their essence is the same.

It is just like the physician's medicines, which might be prepared with different colors and scents to seem different to ordinary people, but the physician, who looks only to their healing power, sees they are the same and is not confused by the additions. In the same way, the man who knows about names looks to their true force, and does not get lost if a letter is added, moved, or even changed entirely, as long as the essence remains.

394b-394e: Returning to Astyanax and Hector

Take the names we just discussed: *Astyanax* and *Hector* — they share hardly any letters but for the tau, yet they express the same meaning. And look at a name like *Archepolis* (ruler of the city), which has none of the same letters yet means precisely the same. There are countless other names for "king," or for "general" — such as *Agis*

48

(leader), *Polemarchus* (war-chief), *Eupolemus* (good warrior) — and names for healers like *Iatrocles* (renowned physician) and *Acesimbrotus* (healer of mortals). Though these names differ in their letters and syllables, they all carry the same essential meaning. Would you agree that this is so?

Hermogenes: Certainly, Socrates.

Socrates: Then those born in accordance with nature ought to receive names that match that nature.

Hermogenes: Yes, absolutely.

Socrates: Then what about those who are born contrary to nature — like prodigies? For instance, when an impious son is born to a good and pious father, should he not, just as we said before of a mare giving birth to a calf, receive the designation that belongs to his true class, rather than that of his parent?

Hermogenes: Certainly, Socrates.

Socrates: So an impious son of a pious father ought to be named according to his true nature.

Hermogenes: True.

Socrates: That means he should not be called *Theophilus* ("beloved of the gods") or *Mnesitheus* ("mindful of the gods"), or anything of that sort — but rather something of opposite meaning, if names are to be truly correct.

Hermogenes: Most assuredly, Socrates.

394e-395e: Mycenaean Myth-Cycle

Socrates: Take Orestes, for example — the name means "mountain man." Whether he got that name by chance or whether some poet chose it to capture his fierce, wild, untamed nature, it was fitting, don't you think?

Hermogenes: Yes, Socrates, that seems clear to me.

Socrates: And Agamemnon, his father's name, also appears to match his true character, in accordance with nature.

Hermogenes: Certainly, Socrates.

Socrates: Yes, Agamemnon means *admirable for remaining*: one who holds firm, determined to complete his task, crowning that resolve with virtue. Look how he endured, holding the host together at Troy year after year. His name rightly honors this power to remain steadfast.

And consider Atreus — it is correct too, if you look beneath the slight disguise of its syllables. His cruel murder of Chrysippus and his savage treatment of

Thyestes brought ruin and devastation (*atēra*) to his own household, and showed a fearless, unyielding nature (*atrestos, ateires*). So though the name is veiled from the casual ear, it still reveals to those with trained logos its truth: Atreus was destructive, stubborn, and fearless, and his name fits him in every sense.

I think Pelops is also properly named. His name suggests one who sees only what is near (*pelas*), for when he murdered Myrtilus to win Hippodameia, he could not foresee the future suffering that would crush his entire line. Eager only for what lay close at hand, he ignored the far-off consequences, and so deserved the name Pelops.

Hermogenes: How is that, Socrates?

Socrates: Because he focused only on the immediate prize, without forethought for the distant legacy of ruin that would follow.

And as for Tantalus, I think anyone would agree his name was rightly given and true to nature — if the stories about him are to be believed.

Hermogenes: And what are those stories?

Socrates: Hermogenes, look how many terrible misfortunes overtook Tantalus — not only the destruction of his country in life, but also, after death, the stone balanced over his head in Hades, *talanteia*, so terribly in tune with his name. It seems as if someone who wished to call him *most burdened* (*talantatos*) twisted the name ever so slightly into Tantalus, just as chance preserved it for us in legend.

395e-396d: Zeus, Cronos, and Hesiod's Genealogy

And consider the name of his father, said to be Zeus — a name full of meaning but hard to perceive, since it sounds almost like a riddle divided into two parts: some say Zēna, others Dia. Yet taken together, they show the god's true nature, just as a name should. For who, after all, is more the giver of life (*zēn*) to all living things than the sovereign and ruler of everything? So he is rightly named through whom (*di' on*) life belongs to every creature. But the name is one name split, Dia and Zēna, revealing its truth to those with trained logos.

And though it might at first seem irreverent to call him the son of Cronus — since *Cronus* in the common hearing suggests stupidity — it actually means something far nobler. For *Kronos* echoes *koros*, not a child, but the pure (*katharon*) and unblemished mind. And Cronus, by tradition, is the son of Uranus — and Uranus is rightly named too, for he lifts our sight toward the heavens (*ourania* from *horaō ta anō*), and the philosophers say such upward gazing clears the mind.

If I could recall the entire lineage of Hesiod, I would gladly keep testing all their names in the same way, to see whether this sudden spirit of name-wisdom that seems to possess me today will hold out, or collapse before the end!

396d-397a: Socrates is Possessed with Inspiration

Hermogenes: Socrates, you sound as if you have become a prophet possessed, speaking oracles from the gods!

Socrates: Yes, Hermogenes, and I am quite convinced this inspiration seized me from Euthyphro of Prospalta. For I spent much of the morning listening to him, and he poured his strange, superhuman wisdom into my ears until it possessed my very soul. So today, I think, we ought to let this inspiration work itself out and complete our investigation of names — to see if we can hold the phalanx of logos steady. But tomorrow, if you and the others agree, we will drive out this spirit and purify ourselves, provided we can find some priest or sophist skilled in the art of such cleansing rites.

Hermogenes: I agree, Socrates — with all my heart — for I am eager to hear the rest of this search for the truth of names.

Episode I

397a-397d: Eternal and Unchanging

Socrates: Very well, Hermogenes. Since we have mapped out our strategy for this investigation, where should we next raise the standard of our inquiry? Where can we discover whether names themselves testify that they were not assigned at random, but possess a certain rightful measure? The names of heroes and men, I suspect, might mislead us; for many of these come from ancestral lines, or — as we mentioned before — they can be altogether unfitting, or offered merely as prayers, like *Eutychides* (fortunate one), *Sosias* (savior), or *Theophilus* (beloved of God). I think we had better lay those aside. Instead, we are more likely to discover proper names among the nature of what is eternal and unchanging, where names were given with the greatest care — perhaps even by some power more divine than any mortal lawgiver.

Hermogenes: I think you are right, Socrates.

Socrates: Then shouldn't we begin with the gods, and see how rightly they are called by their names — if these names preserve the possibility of a common field of truth?

Hermogenes: Yes, Socrates, that seems most reasonable.

Socrates: I suspect something of this kind, Hermogenes. I think that the earliest Hellenes believed in only those gods in whom many foreigners still place their faith today — the sun, the moon, the earth, the stars, and the sky. They saw that all these bodies were always moving in their courses, always running, and from this running nature (*thein*) they called them *theoi*, "gods." Later, once they came to know other gods, they applied the same name to them all. Would you say this seems likely, or not?

Hermogenes: Yes, Socrates, very likely indeed.

Socrates: Then what shall we consider next, to maintain our phalanx of inquiry?

Hermogenes: The spirits, surely.

Socrates: And what do you think the name "spirits" (*daimones*) truly means? See if you think there is anything in what I am about to propose.

Hermogenes: Speak on, Socrates.

Socrates: Do you remember how Hesiod describes the *daimones*?

Hermogenes: I do not recall exactly.

Socrates: Nor that he says a golden race of men was the first born?

Hermogenes: Yes, I remember that.

Socrates: Well, he says of them, "But since fate has now covered this race, they are called holy spirits under the earth, noble, averters of evil, guardians of mortal men."

Hermogenes: And what shall we conclude from that?

Socrates: Well then, Hermogenes, I think Hesiod means that the *golden* race was not literally fashioned out of gold, but that they were good and noble in spirit. A sign of this is that he later calls us of the present day the *iron* race.

Hermogenes: Yes, that seems true, Socrates.

Socrates: And surely, if any person of our own day shows true goodness, Hesiod would say they belong to that golden race, wouldn't he?

Hermogenes: Quite likely, yes.

Socrates: And the good, we would agree, are the wise?

Hermogenes: They are indeed.

Socrates: Then I am convinced, Hermogenes, that Hesiod's word *daimones* points to this wisdom. They were called *daimones* because they were *daēmones*, wise and knowing, for in our older tongue these words were the same. This, I think, is why poets rightly say that when a good man dies, he gains great portion and honor among the dead, becoming a *spirit*, in keeping with the name for wisdom. So, whether in life or in death, every good and wise man is of a spiritual nature and rightly called a *daimon*.

Hermogenes: Yes, Socrates, I am convinced and stand beside you in that. But what about the word *hero*? What is its true sense?

398c-398e: Hero

Socrates: That is simpler to grasp, my friend. The name hero has hardly been changed at all, and comes directly from *eros* — love.

Hermogenes: What do you mean by that?

Socrates: Why, Hermogenes, the heroes were all born from the passion of a god for a mortal woman, or a mortal man for a goddess. If you consider the word *hero* in the older Attic pronunciation, you will see how close it stands to *eros*, the very source of their origin, love itself. That is one reason they were so named.

But there is another possibility: these heroes were wise and powerful with words, skilled in questioning — for *erotan* means to ask questions, and *eirein* is the same as *to speak*. So, when spoken in the Attic dialect I mentioned, their name signals that heroes are questioners, orators, and dialecticians. In other words, the heroic race was a tribe of those who could stand in the phalanx of logos, defending reason through skillful questioning.

398e-399d: Man

That much, I think, is easy to understand. But the origin of the name for *man* — *anthropos* — is more difficult. Can you tell me what it means?

Hermogenes: No, Socrates, I cannot. And even if I could, I think you would find it better than I, so I shall leave it to you.

Socrates: Ah, you trust in the inspiration of Euthyphro, I see.

Hermogenes: Clearly.

Socrates: And rightly so, my friend. For just now a clever thought has struck me, and if I am not careful, before the day is out I may be wiser than I should be. So listen carefully. We must remember that in names, we often add or remove letters, or change the accent, shifting them from phrases to single names. For example, take *Dii Philos* — *dear to Zeus*: to turn this into a name, we drop the second iota, and change the accent from acute to grave, pronouncing it *Diphilus*. In other cases we add letters, or change accents the other way.

Hermogenes: True, Socrates.

Socrates: Then consider this, Hermogenes: the word *anthropos* — *man* — seems to me to have undergone just such a transformation. It was once a whole phrase, but became a noun after a single letter, alpha, was removed, and the accent of the final syllable shifted.

Hermogenes: What do you mean?

Socrates: I mean this. Other animals do not examine, nor reflect upon, nor look upward to what they see. But man, once he has seen — *opope* — then looks upward — *anathrei* — and considers what he has seen. Therefore, of all the living creatures, man alone is rightly called *anthropos*, because he is the one who *looks upward upon what he has seen*. That is the mark of one who strives to form a phalanx of logos, to anchor a common field of truth.

399d-400a: Soul

Hermogenes: Of course. Socrates, may I ask you next about another word?

Socrates: Certainly.

Hermogenes: It seems natural, after speaking of *man*, to go on to the distinction between body and soul.

Socrates: Of course.

Hermogenes: Then let us examine them, as we did the others.

Socrates: So you mean we should inquire into why *soul* — *psyche* — is rightly named, and likewise *body* — *soma*?

Hermogenes: Yes, exactly.

Socrates: Let me speak freely, Hermogenes, and see if this makes sense. It seems to me that those who first gave the name *psyche* had in mind that when present in the body, the soul is the source of life. It grants breath and revives (anapsychei) the body. But when this reviving force fails, the body perishes and comes to its end. So they called it *psyche*, for it gives breath and revival.

But wait a moment — be still with me here. I think I see something that might persuade those like Euthyphro and his followers better. They might scorn the first explanation as mere cheap talk, but perhaps they would honor this next one. Listen and judge.

400a-400b: Anaxagoras and the Soul

Hermogenes: I am listening.

Socrates: Tell me — what is it that upholds and carries the whole nature of the body, so that it lives and moves in harmony?

Hermogenes: Nothing but the soul, Socrates.

Socrates: And do you not accept with Anaxagoras that mind or soul is what orders and governs the entire nature of things?

Hermogenes: Yes, I do.

Socrates: Then it would be quite fitting, I think, to call that force which *carries* and *holds* (*echei*) nature (*physis*) by the name *phuseche*, and this, refined and smoothed out, becomes *psyche*.

Hermogenes: I agree, Socrates — that is a far more precise and scientific explanation.

Socrates: So it seems, my friend — though it is almost laughable how close the name comes to revealing the truth, as if guided by a dialectician who steers the phalanx of logos toward a common field of truth.

400b-400c:The Body and the Orphic Poets

Hermogenes: Now what about the next word, Socrates?

Socrates: You mean *soma*, the body?

Hermogenes: Yes.

Socrates: This word, Hermogenes, can be explained in several ways — even more so if you allow the slightest adjustment. Some say the body is the *sema*, a tomb for the soul, since the soul is thought to be buried in this present life. Others claim it is a *sema*, a sign, because through the body the soul gives signals of its own nature.

But I think, Hermogenes, that the Orphic poets came closest. They saw the soul as paying a kind of penalty, imprisoned within the body, and so the body is the *soma* — the safeguard of the soul, keeping it safe like a prison until its penalty is fulfilled. In this sense, *soma* means "safe-house," and not even a letter needs to be changed to understand that meaning.

Episode II

400d–401a: By Zeus! (Naming Gods)

Hermogenes: I think, Socrates, we have said enough about this class of words. But shall we look at the names of the gods the same way you were just speaking of Zeus, and see what kind of correctness they might have?

Socrates: By Zeus, Hermogenes, if we have any sense at all, we must agree there is a most excellent approach: since we know nothing about the gods — neither their nature nor the names they give themselves — it is clear they use their own true names.

A second good approach is this: as in prayers, we should call them by whatever names and patronymics please them, since we know no others. That, I think, is an admirable custom.

So, if you like, let us first declare to the gods that we do not intend to inquire into their being — since we do not claim we can — but rather into what human beings had in mind when they named them, for there is nothing impious in that.

Hermogenes: You are right, Socrates, and I would like to do that.

401b-402a: Hestia, Lawgiver, and Convention

Socrates: Shall we begin, then, with Hestia, as is the convention?

Hermogenes: That would be right.

Socrates: Then what do you think the name-giver had in mind when he called her Hestia?

Hermogenes: By Zeus, that is no easier than the others.

Socrates: My dear Hermogenes, the first name-givers were not simple men — they were thinkers and skilled speakers.

Hermogenes: And what of them?

Socrates: They are surely the ones who gave names. And even in foreign words, if you look, you can see a meaning. This reveals that the process of naming retains a kind of continuity. Take what we call *ousia* (essence); some call it *esia*, others *osia*. If you think of the second form, it is reasonable that the essence of things should be called *Hestia*; and since we say of what is real it is (*estin*), Hestia would fit that as well.

Apparently, in earlier times, we once called 'essence' (*ousia*) 'it is' (*esia*).

And again, if you look at sacrifices, you will see why the first namegivers named her so: those who called the essence of things 'it is' (*esia*) would naturally make offerings first to Hestia. Others who say 'essence' (*osia*) might agree with Heraclitus, that all things flow and nothing stands still. For them, the force that pushes (*othoun*) is the cause and ruler of all, so it would be rightly called 'essence.'

But let that be, since in truth we know nothing. After Hestia, it is right to consider Rhea and Cronus, although Cronus we already discussed.

But perhaps I am talking nonsense.

Hermogenes: Why, Socrates?

Socrates: My friend, I have thought of a swarm of wisdom.

401e–402d: Heraclitus (Socrates' Head Swarms)

Hermogenes: What is this swarm of wisdom you have found?

Socrates: It might sound rather extravagant, but I think it has some plausibility.

Hermogenes: What is plausible?

Socrates: Hermogenes, I seem to see a kind of vision. I see Heraclitus speaking very ancient words, words as old as the age of Cronus and Rhea — words Homer echoes, too.

Hermogenes: What do you mean?

Socrates: Heraclitus says that all things are in motion and nothing stands still, comparing reality to a river's current, saying you cannot step twice into the same stream.

Hermogenes: Yes, that is true.

Socrates: Well then, don't you think the person who gave to the ancestors of the gods the names Cronus and Rhea had the same thought as Heraclitus? Was it random that both names belonged to rivers? Homer, too, says: 'Ocean is the origin of the gods, and their mother Tethys,' and I think Hesiod says the same. Orpheus adds: 'Fair-flowing Ocean was the first to marry, and he wedded his sister Tethys, daughter of his mother. You see, they all agree and point toward Heraclitus' doctrine.

Hermogenes: That seems reasonable, Socrates; but what about the name *Tethys*?

Socrates: The name nearly explains itself. It is the name of a spring, a little disguised; for what is strained (*diattomenon*) and filtered (*ēthoumenon*) can describe spring water, and Tethys combines those ideas.

Hermogenes: That is clever, Socrates.

Socrates: Of course! But what comes next? We already spoke of Zeus.

402d-403b: Poseidon and Pluto

Hermogenes: Yes.

Socrates: Then let's take up his brothers, Poseidon and Pluto, including Pluto's other name.

Hermogenes: By all means.

Socrates: I think the first person to name Poseidon did so because the sea restrained him in walking and prevented him from advancing, acting as a bond (*desmos*) of his feet (*podōn*). So he called its ruler *Posi-desmos*, Poseidon, with the *epsilon* perhaps for euphony. Or it might come from a different form, if instead of a sigma there were two lambdas, meaning knowing many things (*polla eidos*). Or perhaps, since he shakes the earth, the name comes from *seiein* (to shake), with *pi* and *delta* added.

As for Pluto, he was named as the giver of wealth (*ploutos*), since wealth comes up from below, from the earth. And people think Hades is named from *a-eides* (invisible) and so fear him and prefer to say *Pluto*.

403b-403d: Socrates' Thoughts on Hades

Hermogenes: And what do you think, Socrates?

Socrates: I think people have many false ideas about the power of that god and are too afraid of him. They fear that once dead, they must remain in his realm forever, and that their souls go to him stripped of the body. But these facts — his role and his name — fit together, in my opinion.

Hermogenes: How so?

Socrates: I'll tell you my thought. Which holds an animal more strongly in one place — desire or compulsion?

Hermogenes: Desire, Socrates, far more strongly.

Socrates: Then don't you think many would try to escape Hades if he did not bind them with the strongest bond?

Hermogenes: Surely.

Socrates: And if the strongest bond, then it must be desire, not force?

Hermogenes: Yes, plainly.

Socrates: And there are many desires, yes?

Hermogenes: Yes.

Socrates: So if he uses the strongest bond, it is the strongest desire.

Hermogenes: Yes.

403d-404a: By Zeus! (The Strongest Desire)

Socrates: Is there any desire stronger than the wish to become better by associating with someone?

Hermogenes: No, by Zeus, none stronger.

Socrates: Then this, Hermogenes, must be why no one is willing to come back from there, not even the Sirens; they and everyone else are overcome by his spells, so powerful are the words Hades can speak. In this way he is a perfect sophist, a great benefactor of the souls below, who also sends us blessings from the underworld — for he has abundance there. For this reason he is called Pluto. He will not deal with humans while they are alive, but only accepts their souls once they are purified from bodily evils and desires. That shows real philosophy: he knows that only once purified can they be held by the desire for virtue. But as long as they are disturbed by the body's passions, not even his father

Cronus could hold them, though he used his famous chains.

Hermogenes: That makes sense, Socrates.

Socrates: Yes, Hermogenes, and the lawgiver did not call him *Hades* from *a-eides* (invisible), but from *eidenai* (knowing) all noble things.

404b–406b: Demeter, Hera, and Apollo

Hermogenes: Very well, Socrates. What shall we say of Demeter, Hera, Apollo, Athena, Hephaestus, Ares, and the other gods?

Socrates: Demeter seems to be named from giver (*didousa*) and mother (*mētēr*), since she provides food like a mother. As for Hera, she might have been called that because she is lovely (*eratē*), for tradition says Zeus married her for love; but perhaps the lawgiver had in mind natural elements, disguising *air* (*aēr*) by moving the first letter to the end — you'll see what I mean if you repeat Hera several times.

And look at *Pherephatta* — so many people fear that name, just as they do Apollo's, because they do not understand the correctness of names. They transform it to *Persephone* and that frightens them, though really it means the goddess is wise. Since all things are in motion (*pheromena*), what grasps (*ephaptomenon*) and follows them shows wisdom; so *Pherepapha* would be the right name, since she lays hold of what moves, showing wisdom. That is why wise Hades consorts with her. But people change the name for the sake of smoothness, calling her *Pherephatta* instead of the truth.

Similarly with Apollo: many fear his name, thinking it means something terrible.

Hermogenes: Yes, that's true.

Socrates: But actually, the name is beautifully suited to the god's power.

Hermogenes: How so?

Socrates: Let me try to explain. No single name could better capture the four roles of Apollo — music, prophecy, medicine, and archery. In medicine, prophecy, and ritual, there are purifications, cleansings, fumigations, sprinklings — all meant to purify body and soul.

Hermogenes: Yes, of course.

Socrates: And Apollo is the god who purifies and frees us from such evils. So in terms of washing away and releasing, he might be called *Apoluon* (the cleanser, the absolver). In terms of prophecy and truth, which is simple and direct, the Thessalians call him *Aploun* (simple, sincere). As a bowman, he is ever shooting (*aei ballōn*), and musically, the alpha in his name can mean together, suggesting harmony — moving things together as the astronomers and musicians say the heavens do. Apollo guides this harmony among gods and men alike.

So, just as words like *akolouthos* (companion) and *akoitis* (bedmate) replace *homo-* with *a-*, the name *Apollon* replaces *homopolon*, with an extra lambda to avoid the sound of *apolō* (to destroy). Even so, some people fear this god's name because they think it means ruin, not seeing its real sense: that it brings together cleansing, truth, archery, and harmony.

As for the Muses and music generally, their name seems to come from *mōsthai* (to search, inquire), which links them to philosophy. Leto may be called that because she is gentle and willing (*ethelemon*), granting what people ask; or maybe foreigners who call her *Letho* refer to her calm and mild nature (*leion*).

Artemis seems to get her name from her soundness and healthy character (*artemēs*), or perhaps from being skilled in virtue (*arete*), or because she hates intercourse (*aroton misei*). Whoever gave the name may have meant any or all of these things.

406b-406d: Dionysus and Aphrodite

Hermogenes: What of Dionysus and Aphrodite?

Socrates: Ah, you ask a lot of me, my friend! Well, there is a serious explanation of their names, but also a playful one — for even the gods enjoy a jest. Dionysus could be *Didoinysus*, the giver (*didous*) of wine (*oinos*), and wine itself, since it makes drinkers think (*oiesthai*) they have intelligence (*nous*) when they don't, might jokingly be called *Oeonus* (mind-wine). As for Aphrodite, there's no reason to reject Hesiod's story that her name comes from being born of the foam (*aphros*).

406d-407d: Athena, Hephaestus, and Ares

Hermogenes: And what about Athena, and Hephaestus, and Ares? You surely won't forget them, as an Athenian.

Socrates: No, of course not. It's easy enough to explain one of Athena's two names.

Hermogenes: Which one?

Socrates: Pallas.

Hermogenes: Yes.

Socrates: I think those are right who say this comes from armed dancing, because to leap or lift something off the ground with the hands is called *pallein*, to shake or to brandish.

Hermogenes: That makes sense.

Socrates: So that explains Pallas.

Hermogenes: And what of her other name?

Socrates: You mean Athena? That is more difficult. The ancients seem to have thought of her as the *mind* or *intellect* (nous, dianoia), and the name-giver gave her an even more grand title: divine mind (*theonoe*). He seems to have changed the vowels a bit, dropping iota and sigma, making it sound like *Athena*. Or perhaps it refers to moral intelligence (*ethonoe*), wisdom in character, which was later refined to Athena.

Hermogenes: What about Hephaestus?

Socrates: You mean the master of shining light? His name is simply *Phaestus*, with an *eta* added by attraction.

Hermogenes: Reasonable — unless you find something else.

Socrates: To avoid that risk, ask me about Ares!

Hermogenes: All right, what of Ares?

Socrates: Well, he could be named from *arren*, male, showing strength and manliness, or from *arratos*, hard, unbending, which fits the god of war.

Hermogenes: That seems good.

407d-408d: By the Gods! By Zeus! (Hermogenes)

Socrates: By the gods, let's leave off the gods — I'm afraid to talk about them! Ask me about anything else you wish — that you may see what Euthyphro's horses are worth.

Hermogenes: Just one more god, Socrates — Hermes. Cratylus says I'm not really a son of Hermes. Let's look at the name.

Socrates: Right. Well, Hermes seems linked to speech, as interpreter (*hermeneus*), messenger, clever talker. All of that is about language. The verb *eirein* means to speak, and Homer uses *emesato* (he contrived) often. So the name could come from he who contrived speech (*eirein emesato*), and the lawgiver might have told us: Call him Eiremes. But we beautified it into Hermes. Iris too seems named from *eirein*, since she is a messenger.

Hermogenes: By Zeus, Cratylus was right that I'm no Hermogenes — I'm no good at speaking!

Socrates: It also makes sense, my friend, that Pan is the double-natured son of Hermes.

Hermogenes: How so?

Socrates: Because speech (*logos*) reveals everything (*pan*), moves it about, and has two forms, truth and falsehood.

Hermogenes: True.

Socrates: The true part is smooth, divine, living with the gods, while falsehood lives among men, rough and goatlike — just like the tragic goat. Stories and lies belong to that tragic, goatish world.

Hermogenes: Yes, exactly.

Socrates: So Pan, who reveals and moves everything (*aei polōn*), is rightly called goat-herd (*aipolos*), the two-natured son of Hermes: smooth above, rough and goatlike below. And if he is Hermes' son, he is speech or its brother — and it is no surprise that brother resembles brother. But, as I said, let's get away from the gods now, my friend.

Episode III

408d–409c: Sun and Moon, and Month and Stars

Hermogenes: Well then, Socrates, if you like, let's leave those gods aside. But why shouldn't we talk about other gods — like the sun, moon, stars, earth, aether, air, fire, water, the seasons, and the year?

Socrates: You are putting a lot on my shoulders! But if it pleases you, I'm willing.

Hermogenes: It will please me very much.

Socrates: All right. Where shall we begin? With the sun, since you mentioned it first?

Hermogenes: Yes, let's.

Socrates: It may be clearer to look at its Doric form. The Dorians say *Halios* for the sun. That might come from *alizein*, to gather, because when he rises he gathers people together. Or it might come from *aei eilein*, always turning around the earth, or from *aiolein*, which means variegate, since the sun colors and variegates the products of the earth.

Hermogenes: And what about the moon — Selene?

Socrates: That name rather upsets Anaxagoras!

Hermogenes: Why so?

Socrates: Because the name *Selene* seems to have anticipated Anaxagoras' theory that the moon receives its light from the sun.

Hermogenes: How so?

Socrates: *Selas* (gleam) and *phos* (light) really mean the same.

Hermogenes: Yes.

Socrates: And if Anaxagoras is right, the moon always has both new and old light — the sun continually refreshes it, while the leftover light from the previous month remains.

Hermogenes: That makes sense.

Socrates: Sometimes the moon is called *Selanaia*.

Hermogenes: True.

Socrates: Since she has new and old gleam (*selas neon kai henon*), the best name would be *Selaneoneoaia*, which people compressed into *Selanaia*.

Hermogenes: That's quite a comic opera name, Socrates! What about the month and the stars?

Socrates: The word for month, *meis*, comes from *meiousthai*, to grow less, as the month wanes. And the stars, *asteres*, come from *astrape* (lightning). But *astrape*, because it turns the eyes upward (*anastrephein*), would properly be *anastrope*, which got refined into *astrape*.

409d-410c: By Zeus! (Socrates' Machina)

Hermogenes: What about fire and water?

Socrates: Fire (*pyr*) defeats me. Either the Muse of Euthyphro has deserted me, or it is a very tough word. So let me show you my method for these difficult cases.

Hermogenes: What method?

Socrates: I will explain. But first, do you know the reason for the word *pyr*?

Hermogenes: By Zeus, no!

Socrates: Then see what I suspect: many Greeks, especially those living under barbarian rule, borrowed words from them.

Hermogenes: Yes, and?

Socrates: If we try to explain these words as purely Greek, instead of from their foreign source, we will be misled.

Hermogenes: Naturally.

Socrates: So I suspect *pyr* is foreign. It is hard to relate to Greek, and the Phrygians have a similar word. The same goes for *hydor* (water), *kyon* (dog), and many others.

Hermogenes: That's fair.

Socrates: So let's leave *pyr* and *hydor* aside rather than force them. As for *aer* (air), it might come from *airein* (to raise up) or *aei rei* (always flowing), or because the winds arise from its flowing. Poets sometimes call the winds *aetai* (blasts), meaning *air-flow* (*aetorroun*) just as you might say *wind-flow* (*pneumatorroun*).

Hermogenes: And *aether*?

Socrates: It might be *aeitheer*, because it always moves and flows around the air (*aei thei peri ton aera reon*).

Hermogenes: And *earth*?

Socrates: The word *gē* is clearer in the form *gaia*, which means mother, as Homer uses *gegaasi* for to be born.

Hermogenes: Good.

410c-410e: Seasons and Year

Socrates: Next?

Hermogenes: The seasons and the year.

Socrates: The seasons, *horai*, should be spelled in the older Attic way, *horai*, because they divide (*horizousi*) the summer and winter, the winds, and the harvests. As for the two words for year, *eniautos* and *etos*: they really come from the same idea. That which brings forth all plants and animals in due season, and reviews them within itself, is called *eniautos* from *en eauto* (in itself), and *etos* from *etazein* (to examine), just as we divided the name of Zeus into *Dia* and *Zena*. So these two words really split apart one idea: that which examines within itself.

Hermogenes: Truly, Socrates, you are going at a tremendous speed!

Socrates: Yes — I think I have already come quite far on this road of wisdom.

Hermogenes: I believe you have.

Socrates: And you'll believe it even more in a moment.

411a-413d: Words Tied to Virtue

Hermogenes: Now that you've explained that class of words, I'd like us to examine the noble words tied to virtue — like wisdom, intelligence, justice, and others of that kind.

Socrates: Ah, you're stirring up quite a tribe of words, my friend! But since I have already put on the lion's helmet, I mustn't turn coward. Let's look at wisdom, intelligence, thought, knowledge, and all the other grand-sounding words.

Hermogenes: We cannot stop until we do.

Socrates: By the dog, I just had an insight! I think those ancient name-makers were rather like today's philosophers: they get dizzy as they spin around looking for the nature of things, and then the things themselves seem to spin and flow and move. They think that it's not their own confusion but that the world is really in constant flux — nothing standing still, everything flowing, moving, being generated. That is why they named things as they did.

Hermogenes: What do you mean?

Socrates: You may not have noticed, but all these words are given on the assumption that what they name is in motion, flowing, being generated.

Hermogenes: I didn't see that.

Socrates: Let's look at *phronesis* — wisdom. Its name seems to mean *perception* (*noesis*) of motion (*phoras*) and flow (*rhou*), or perhaps *the blessing* (*onesis*) of motion — in either case, tied to movement. As for *gnome* — judgment — that surely points to *reflecting* and *considering* generation (*gones nomes*), since to consider is to reflect. Or, if you like, *noesis* might mean *the longing (esis) for the new (neou)*, since what is new is always coming into being. So the soul's desire for fresh generation was marked by the ancient name *neoesis* — though later the double epsilon was replaced by an eta.

Sophrosyne — self-restraint — could then be seen as the *salvation* (*soteria*) of wisdom, preserving the very movement of mind we just discussed.

Episteme — knowledge — signals that the soul worthy of anything *follows along with* (*epetai*) the movement of things, neither lagging behind nor racing ahead. That is why some think it should properly be *epistemene*, with an epsilon added.

Sunesis — intelligence — is a kind of *gathering together*, a reckoning, since to "understand" (*sunienai*) is much the same as to *know*, and means the soul proceeds in harmony with things.

And *sophia* — wisdom — is the most hidden of these. It seems to come from elsewhere, a foreign word. But poets speak of a thing setting out swiftly as *esuthe* — "it rushed" — and there was a famous Spartan named *Sous*, for the Spartans called swift movement by that name. So *sophia* could mean *the touch* (*epaphe*) of swift movement, assuming all things are in motion.

Finally, *agathon* — the good — points to what is admirable (*agaston*) in nature. Since all things move, they have their degrees of quickness or slowness; but not all speed is admirable. Only the admirable (*agaston*) element within that swiftness deserves to be called *agathon*, the good.

Justice — *dikaiosyne* — seems easy enough to break down as *the understanding* (*sunesis*) of what is just (*tou diaiou*). But the very word *dikaion* itself is far harder to untangle. Up to a point, most people seem to agree about what it means, but beyond that they split apart.

See, those who believe all things are in motion claim that most of the cosmos is merely a receptacle — a vessel — and that through this vessel passes a certain element, subtle and swift, by which all things are generated. This element must be exceedingly fine, so nothing can resist it, and exceedingly fast, so that other things seem at rest by comparison. Since it *passes through* (*diaion*) and oversees all things, they say it is rightly named *dikaion* — with a kappa inserted only for the sake of sound. Up to this point, as I have told you, there is some agreement about justice.

But I, Hermogenes, being deeply dedicated to understanding, have asked again and again — and certain teachers told me in a kind of sacred whisper that justice is not only this, but is itself the *cause* of things, for it is through this element that creation takes place. Some even claimed that for this reason it is rightly named *Zeus* (*Dia*).

Yet when I quietly press them, asking "But tell me plainly, friend, what then is justice?" they scold me for being a nuisance and for leaping too far beyond their explanations. They say they have told me enough, and begin contradicting one another. One claims justice is the sun, for the sun alone passes through and burns (*diaionta kai kaionta*) everything, overseeing it all.

Then I, delighted, repeat this to someone else — but he laughs and says, "Then does justice vanish the moment the sun sets?" So I beg him to tell me what he believes, and he says, "It is fire." But then he adds, "Not actual fire, but abstract heat present in the fire," which is even harder to grasp.

Another dismisses them all and says, like Anaxagoras, that justice is *mind* — for mind alone commands itself, mixes with nothing, governs everything, and passes through all things.

So in the end, my friend, I am more bewildered about justice than I was before I began searching. But for the name itself — that, I still believe, was given for the reasons I have explained.

413d-414b: Courage

Hermogenes: I'm sure you didn't make this up on your own!

Socrates: And how about the rest of my talk?

Hermogenes: That part, I do believe was yours!

Socrates: Very well, then, listen to me again — though perhaps I may fool you into thinking all these thoughts are my own. What remains for us to examine after justice? Surely we have not yet spoken of courage (*andreia*). As for *adikia* (injustice), that is simple enough, since it is no more than a blockage or hindrance to that which should pass through (*tou diaiontos*), and need not detain us.

But *andreia*, courage, suggests a certain struggle or contest, for if the universe is in constant flow, then a battle within it would be a counterflow (*enantia rhoe*). If we remove the delta from *andreia*, we are left with *anreia*, which points to precisely this kind of opposition. Yet, of course, it is not a current opposed to every current that is praised as courage, but only the one that opposes the current contrary to justice — for otherwise we would not hold courage in honor.

And consider, too, the words *arren* (male) and *aner* (man); they seem to echo the same sense of upward-flow (*ano rhoe*). The word *gune* (woman) appears related to *gone* (birth), which is fitting. And as for *thelu* (female), I think it takes its name from *thele* (the teat), which is so called because it makes things flourish (*tethelenai*), just as plants grow and blossom when refreshed by rain.

Hermogenes: That does seem quite likely, Socrates.

Socrates: And look further, Hermogenes: the word *thallein* — "to flourish" — appears to express the sudden, vigorous growth of the young. The namegiver, I think, captured this sense by weaving together *thein* (to run) and *allesthai* (to leap). You see, I cannot help but race on, galloping far beyond the marked course, whenever I find smooth ground underfoot!

But still, there are many more words remaining that are held to be weighty and deserving of our inquiry.

Hermogenes: Yes, indeed, Socrates.

414b-414d: Techne

Socrates: All right — then let's look at the word techne (art, craft, skill).

Hermogenes: Yes, let's do that.

Socrates: Doesn't it suggest *possession of mind* if you remove the tau and slip in an omicron between the chi and the nu, and another omicron between the nu and eta — making it echonoe?

Hermogenes: That is a very poor explanation, Socrates.

Socrates: My dear friend, you forget how the original forms of words have long been buried by those who tried to embellish them. They added and removed letters to please the ear, twisting them around for style or for ornament, or simply through the passage of time. Haven't you noticed, for example, how absurd it is that there's a rho in the word katoptron (mirror)? That seems to me the work of people who cared nothing for truth, but only for shaping their mouths nicely. They kept adding to the old words until no human being could make out what they ever meant. Or look at sphinx, which ought to be phix — there are many such cases.

Hermogenes: Yes, that is true, Socrates.

Socrates: And if people are allowed to stick in or strip out letters wherever they please, then of course any name can be made to match any object.

Hermogenes: That's quite true.

Socrates: Yes, exactly — so you, as a wise guide, must stick to moderation and reason.

Hermogenes: I would like to do that.

414e-415e: The Summit of Mechane

Socrates: And I share that feeling, Hermogenes. But, my friend, do not ask for too strict a precision, lest you, as Homer says, *"enfeeble me of my sight."* Now that *technē* (art) has been considered, let us move onward to what I see as the very summit of our discussion, once we have examined *mēkhanē* (contrivance). I suspect this word suggests *anein epi polu* — a great accomplishment — since *mēkos* (length) can mean something great, and the name is formed from these elements, *mēkos* and *anein*.

Yet now, as I climb toward the heights, let us turn to the words *aretē* (virtue) and *kakia* (vice). One of these, *kakia*, is easier to see, and seems to fit with all we have argued before. Since everything is in motion, anything that moves poorly (*kakōs iōn*) is evil, and when this kind of evil movement infects the soul, it earns the special name *kakia* — vice.

The nature of this evil motion, I think, is shown as well by the word *deilia* (cowardice), which we should have explored right after *andreia* (courage), but we overlooked it — as we may have done with other words. *Deilia* seems to mean a powerful bond upon the soul, since *lian* expresses strength, so that *deilia* is the greatest *desmos* (bond) binding the soul. Similarly, *aporia* (perplexity) is an evil, for it blocks and frustrates advance and movement (*poreuesthai*).

Thus, it seems that evil motion is a stumbling and obstructed advance, which fills the soul with vice. And if that is the reason behind *kakia*, then *aretē* would be its opposite: first, it means freedom of motion; then, that the current of the good soul proceeds without impediment, always flowing (*aei rheon*) and unblocked — hence it gains its name as *aeireitē*, or even *hairetē*, as something to be especially chosen. But compressed in sound, it is called *aretē*.

You might suspect I am making all of this up again, but if my explanation of *kakia* was correct, then this, too, must be sound.

416a-416d: By Zeus! (Foreign Origins of Roots)

Hermogenes: But, Socrates, what about the word *kakon* (evil), which you have been using in so many of these derivations — what does it mean?

Socrates: By Zeus, that word is a strange one, Hermogenes, and very hard to get at. So here, as before, I will fall back on my usual contrivance.

Hermogenes: And what contrivance is that?

Socrates: To suggest that it is of foreign origin — the same explanation I have given for other obscure words.

Hermogenes: That is probably right. But if you agree, let us set aside these words and see if we can discover the reasons behind *kalon* (noble, beautiful) and *aischron* (base).

Socrates: I think the meaning of *aischron* is quite plain, and it also fits with everything we have been saying. For the name-giver seems, throughout, to wage war on anything that blocks or restrains the natural flow. In this case, he gave the name *aeischoroun* to that which "always holds back the flow" (*aei ischon ton rhoun*), which over time has been contracted and spoken as *aischron*.

Hermogenes: And what about *kalon*?

Socrates: That is more obscure. But it also conveys its sense, after a shift of accent and vowel length.

Hermogenes: Explain how.

Socrates: Well, what do you suppose is the true cause of something having a name? Is it not the power that gives it its name?

Hermogenes: Of course.

Socrates: And that power is the *nous* — the intellect — whether of gods or men or both?

Hermogenes: Yes.

Socrates: So what gives names — *to kaloun* — is intellect, the same faculty that calls things by their proper name?

Hermogenes: That is clear.

Socrates: And all works produced by intelligence and understanding are praiseworthy, while those produced without them are blameworthy?

Hermogenes: Yes, certainly.

Socrates: A doctor produces medical works, and a carpenter carpentry works, right?

Hermogenes: Yes.

Socrates: Then the *beautiful* produces works of beauty?

Hermogenes: It must.

Socrates: And *the beautiful*, we say, is the work of intellect?

Hermogenes: Yes.

Socrates: Therefore the name *kalon* is properly given to intellect, since it achieves the works that we praise as beautiful.

Hermogenes: That seems reasonable.

416e-417c: The Good and the Beautiful

Socrates: Then what other words do we still have to examine?

Hermogenes: The ones connected with the good and the beautiful: *sumpheron* (advantageous), *lusiteloun* (profitable), *ophelimon* (useful), *kerdaleon* (gainful), and their opposites.

Socrates: By now, Hermogenes, I think you could work out for yourself what *sumpheronta* (useful, advantageous) means, if you keep in mind everything we have said so far. It is, in a way, the sister of *episteme* (knowledge), pointing to the soul's motion (*phora*) carried along in harmony with the movement of the world. Naturally, then, things which follow and are borne along with this cosmic motion are called *sumphora* or *sumpheronta* because they are "carried together" (*sumperephesthai*) with the flow of all things.

As for *kerdaleon* (profitable), it comes from *kerdos* (gain). If you were to swap a nu for the delta in *kerdos*, the meaning would become plain — it indicates something good in a different way, since it "mingles" (*kerannytai*) with all things and passes through them. The name-giver made this intention clear by choosing that form, though he replaced nu with delta and settled on *kerdos*.

Hermogenes: And how about *lusiteloun* (profitable)?

Socrates: Well, I think the name-giver did not mean the everyday sense tradesmen use — where profit sets free their investment. Rather, he saw profit as the thing that is fastest of all, which refuses to let things come to rest, never lets motion reach its end (*telos*), but whenever there is any pause or conclusion, it loosens it again, making movement endless and immortal. So he called the good *lusiteloun*, meaning it loosens (*lyei*) the *end* (*telos*) of motion.

Hermogenes: That is clever. And *ophelimon*?

Socrates: *Ophelimon* is actually a foreign word, which Homer often uses in the sense of *ophellein* — to increase or to make grow.

417d-419b: Opposite of Good and Profitable

Hermogenes: What, Socrates, shall we say of the opposites of these good and profitable things?

Socrates: For those that are simply negatives, Hermogenes, I think they hardly need any special explanation.

Hermogenes: Which do you mean?

Socrates: Words like *unprofitable*, *disadvantageous*, *unhelpful*, and *ungainful*.

Hermogenes: That seems fair.

Socrates: But let us look more closely at words like *blaberon* (harmful) and *zemiodes* (hurtful).

Hermogenes; Yes, please.

Socrates: *Blaberon* is really the name for whatever harms or interrupts (*blapton*) the flow (*roun*) of things. Now *blapton* itself means "desiring to fasten" (*haptein*) the stream — and *haptein* is just another way of saying "to bind" (*dein*), which, as you remember, the name-giver consistently criticizes as something constraining. So the phrase "that which wishes to bind the flow" (*boulomenon haptein roun*) would, if expressed with perfect precision, have been *boulapteroun*. But to soften the sound, people call it *blaberon* instead.

Hermogenes: Socrates, those are rather elaborate names you are forging — just now, when you said *boulapteroun*, I thought you were about to puff up and sing the flute-prelude to Athena's hymn!

Socrates: Not my fault, Hermogenes — blame the name-givers.

Hermogenes: That's true. But what about *zēmiōdes*? How does that word work?

Socrates: What about *zēmiōdes*? Well, Hermogenes, notice what I said earlier — how true it is that just by adding or taking away a letter, people can completely change the sense of a word. Even the tiniest change can flip its meaning to the opposite. Take the word *deon*, for example. It just came to mind while I was talking to you. This flashy modern language of ours has twisted *deon* — and *zēmiōdes* too — around so much that both words now mean nearly the opposite of what they originally showed. But the older language makes their meanings perfectly clear.

Hermogenes: What do you mean?

Socrates: I'll explain. You know how our ancestors valued the sounds of *iota* and *delta* — especially the women, who were the strongest at keeping the old ways of speaking. But nowadays people change *iota* to *eta* or *epsilon*, and *delta* to *zeta*, because they think it sounds fancier.

Hermogenes: How do you mean?

Socrates: Well, for example, in the very earliest days they used to call the day *imera*, while some said *emera*, and nowadays we say *hemera*.

Hermogenes: That's true.

Socrates: But only the ancient word really shows what the name-giver had in mind, don't you see? Because day comes to people after darkness, and they welcome it, they *long* for it — *imeirousi* — so they called it *imera*.

Hermogenes: That makes sense.

Socrates: But now the word *hemera* is so changed around that you couldn't even guess its meaning. In fact, some people think the word *hemera* comes from making things gentle (*hemera* with a different accent).

Hermogenes: I think they do.

Socrates: And you know the old word for 'yoke' was *duogon*.

Hermogenes: Of course.

Socrates: But *zugon* doesn't really tell you anything — it's *duogon* that properly describes something that brings two together for pulling. But now we say *zugon* instead. There are plenty of other words that have shifted like this.

Hermogenes: Yes, that's obvious.

Socrates: And in the same way, look at the word *deon* (obligation): the way they said it at first shows almost the opposite of what all the other words for good express. Because even though *deon* is a kind of good, it also acts as a kind of chain — a *desmos* — and a hindrance to movement, almost like a brother to *blaberon* (harmful).

Hermogenes: Yes, Socrates, that seems very clear.

Socrates: But that's not so, if you go back to the older form of the word, which is probably more correct. If you put back the *iota* instead of the *epsilon*, the way they used to, then you get *dion* instead of *deon*. That word fits with the other words for 'good,' because *dion* — not *deon* — actually means something good, something that the name-giver praises. So the name-maker isn't contradicting himself, but is consistent with all these other names: *deon* (obligation), *ophelimon* (useful), *lusiteloun* (profitable), *kerdaleon* (gainful), *agathon* (good), *sumpheron* (advantageous), and *euporon* (plentiful) — all these describe, in different ways, the principle of arrangement and motion, which people have always praised, while the principle of restriction and bondage is always criticized.

And the same is true with *zemiodes* (harmful): if you change the *zeta* back to a *delta*, like in the old speech, you get *demiodes*, which was meant to name something that binds or ties down movement — *dounti to ion*.

419b-420b: Pleasure, Pain, and Desire

Hermogenes: What about words like *hedone* (pleasure), *lupe* (pain), and *epithumia* (desire), Socrates?

Socrates: I don't think these are difficult at all, Hermogenes. Take *hedone* (pleasure): it seems to have that name because it is an activity that moves toward benefit — *he pros ten onesin teinousa* — but a *delta* got inserted along the way, so people now say *hedone* instead of the older *heone*.

As for *lupe* (pain), it probably got its name from the loosening or breaking down (*diolysis*) of the body that comes with pain. *Ania* (trouble or sorrow) comes from something that blocks or hinders movement — it stops the going (*ienai*).

Algedon (distress), I think, is a foreign borrowing from *algeinos* (painful). *Odune* (grief) seems to come from the 'putting on' of pain — *endusis tes lupes*. *Achthedon* (vexation) got its name from being like a weight (*achthos*) that burdens movement, which anyone can see.

Chara (joy) appears to be named for the wide spreading or pouring out (*diachysis*) of the soul's current. *Terpsis* (delight) comes from *terpnon* (delightful), and that goes back to the creeping movement (*herpsis*) of the soul, which is compared to a breath (*pnoe*) — properly it should have been called *herpnoun*, but over time it became *terpnon*.

Euphrosyne (cheerfulness) really doesn't need much explaining, because clearly it comes from the soul moving in harmony (*eu*) with the natural order, so its true form was *eupherosyne*, but it has ended up as *euphrosyne*.

And *epithumia* (desire) is not hard either: its name plainly points to a power that goes (*iousa*) into the *thumos* (soul's spirited part). And *thumos* itself is named after the boiling or seething (*thysis*) of the soul.

Himeros (longing) comes from a flow (*rous*) that draws the soul the strongest; since it flows with a rush (*iemenos*) and pulls the soul along with that rushing desire, people named it *himeros*.

Pothos (yearning) means something whose object is not present, but somewhere else (*allothi pou*) — so the same passion is called *himeros* when its object is present, but *pothos* when the object is absent.

Eros (love) is called that because it flows inward (*esrei*) from the outside — this flow is not inherent in the lover but comes in through the eyes. That is why the ancients called it *esros*, from *esrein*, using *omicron* instead of *omega* back then, but today it is called *eros* because *omega* replaced *omicron*.

So — is there anything else you want to examine?

420b-420c: Opinion

Hermogenes: What about *doxa* (opinion) and those kinds of words?

Socrates: Well, *doxa* might come from *dioxis* (pursuit), describing how the soul chases after knowledge of the nature of things — or it might come from *toxon* (a bow), which is probably more correct. And the word *oiesis* (belief) supports that second option, since *oiesis* seems to mean the movement (*oisis*) of the soul toward the real nature of each thing, just like *boule* (counsel) comes from *bole* (a throwing or shooting), and *boulesthai* (to wish or plan) includes the sense of aiming at something.

So these words all seem to follow the pattern of *doxa*, expressing the idea of shooting at a target. And on the other side, *aboulia* (lack of counsel or confusion) suggests a failure — as if someone didn't hit or even aim correctly at what they wished, planned, or intended.

420d-420e: Socrates' Final Lap

Hermogenes: You're picking up speed, Socrates.

Socrates: Yes — I'm finishing up, running my final lap, so to speak. But I still think I should explain *anagke* (necessity or compulsion) and *hekousion* (voluntary), since they naturally come next.

The word *hekousion* seems to point to yielding (*eikon*) and not resisting — that is, giving way to a movement that matches the will. But *anagkaion* (what is necessary or compulsory), being opposed to our will, is connected to error and ignorance. It's like making your way through a ravine (*anke*), which is hard to pass through, rough, and tangled, and slows down movement; so the word *anagkaion* might come from the idea of going through a ravine (*an anke ion*).

But as long as I have any energy left, I won't stop, and don't you stop asking me questions either.

420e-421c: Greatest and Most Noble Words

Hermogenes: All right then — let me ask about the greatest and most important words: truth (*aletheia*), falsehood (*pseudos*), being (*to on*), and why name (*onoma*), which is the whole focus of our conversation, is called *onoma*.

Socrates: Tell me — do you know the word *mai-esthai*?

Hermogenes: Yes — it means 'to seek.'

Socrates: The word *onoma* (name) seems to come from a whole compressed phrase meaning 'this is a being about which there is a search.' You can see that even more clearly in the adjective *onomaston* (notable), because that plainly shows *on ou masma estin* — 'a being for which there is a searching.'

And *aletheia* (truth) is similar. I think the divine motion of the cosmos is called *aletheia* because it is a divine wandering — *theia ale*.

But *pseudos* (falsehood) is the opposite of movement: once again, anything forced to stand still, to be quiet and inactive, is seen as something blameworthy, and it is compared to people who are sleeping (*heuousi*); the addition of the 'psi' hides this meaning.

As for *on* (being) and *ousia* (essence or existence), they connect to *aletheia* too, since they really come from *ion* ('going') with the iota lost. *On* means 'going,' and *ouk on* (not being) means *ouk ion* (not going), and in fact some people even pronounce it that way.

421c-422c: The Foreign Roots

Hermogenes: Well, Socrates, you have smashed these words apart with real courage — but suppose someone asked you what justification or correctness there is for these roots you're using, like *ion*, *reon*, or *doun* — how would you prove they're really fitting?

Socrates: So you're asking what kind of answer I could give him — is that what you mean?

Hermogenes: Yes, exactly.

Socrates: Well, we came up with a way just now to give a kind of answer that at least seems reasonable.

Hermogenes: What way was that?

Socrates: By saying that any name whose meaning we cannot figure out is probably of foreign origin. That might actually be true in some cases. And also, because of how much time has passed, it may be impossible to trace back the oldest words; after all, words get twisted and reshaped in so many ways over time, that I wouldn't be surprised if an ancient Greek word ended up being exactly the same as a word from some other language today.

Hermogenes: That does seem pretty likely.

Socrates: Yes, that's pretty likely. Still, we should take this investigation seriously and not hold back. Remember, if someone keeps on asking about the words from which names are formed, and then about the words from which *those* words come, and continues indefinitely, the person answering will eventually give up, don't you think?

Hermogenes: Yes, I think so.

Socrates: So when would it be reasonable for him to stop and give up? Wouldn't it be when he finally reaches the names that are the elements of all the other names and words? Because if these are elements, then they can no longer properly be broken down into smaller names.

For example, we just said that *agathon* (good) was made from *agaston* (admirable) and *thoos* (swift); and maybe you could say *thoos* comes from other elements, and those from still others. But if at some point you come to a word that can't be broken down any further, then it would be right to say you've reached an element, and you don't have to look for its derivation in other words anymore.

Hermogenes: Yes, that seems right to me.

Socrates: Well then, do you think these words we're talking about now might actually be such elements — and that we should test their correctness by some other method?

Hermogenes: Probably.

Socrates: Yes, probably, Hermogenes. After all, everything we've analyzed so far leads back to these. And if that's really true — as I think it is — please stay with me and help me look carefully, so I don't end up saying something ridiculous about what principle lies behind the correctness of the very first names.

Hermogenes: Go ahead — I'll help as much as I can.

Socrates: I think you'd agree with me, Hermogenes, that there is a single standard of correctness for all names — the earliest and the latest alike — and that no name is more truly a name than any other.

Hermogenes: Yes, absolutely.

422d-423b: The Nature of the Thing

Socrates: And the correctness of all these names, as we've seen, is about showing the nature of the things they name.

Hermogenes: Of course.

Socrates: So that principle has to be present in every name, whether it's one of the earliest or one of the later ones, if it is to count as a genuine name.

Hermogenes: Definitely.

Socrates: Now it seems that the later names were able to do this by means of the earlier ones.

Hermogenes: That makes sense.

Socrates: But what about the very first names — those that weren't built on any other words? How could they possibly reveal the nature of things, which they have to do if they are going to be real names? Tell me this: if people had no voice or tongue, but still wanted to communicate, wouldn't they, just like mute people do, try to make signs with their hands, their heads, and their whole bodies?

Hermogenes: Yes — what other option is there, Socrates?

Socrates: Well, if we wanted to show something above us, something light, I suppose we would lift our hand up toward the sky, trying to match the nature of the thing. If it was something below or heavy, we would push our hands down toward the earth. And if we wanted to refer to a galloping horse or any other animal, we'd try to make our body mimic theirs as closely as possible.

Hermogenes: Yes, I agree, there's no other way.

Socrates: So it seems that to express anything at all, the body would imitate the thing it wants to show.

Hermogenes: Yes.

Socrates: And when we use voice, tongue, or mouth to express something, wouldn't it be the same — wouldn't they indicate what they mean through imitation too?

Hermogenes: That seems unavoidable.

423c-425a: By Zeus! (Vocal Imitations)

Socrates: Then it would seem that a name is a kind of vocal imitation of what it tries to name, and someone who imitates something with their voice is naming it.

Hermogenes: That sounds right.

Socrates: By Zeus, I'm not sure that is fully right, my friend.

Hermogenes: Why not?

Socrates: Well, we'd have to admit that people who copy the sounds of goats or roosters or other animals were actually naming them.

Hermogenes: Yes, I guess we would have to.

Socrates: Do you think that's correct?

Hermogenes: No, I don't. So, Socrates — what sort of imitation is a name, then?

Socrates: First of all, Hermogenes, I don't think we'd really be making names if we just imitated things the way music does — even though musical imitation uses the voice, too. And I also don't think we'd be naming anything by copying what music itself imitates.

Here's what I mean: everything has a sound and a shape, and many things have color, right?

Hermogenes: Yes, of course.

Socrates: But the art of naming doesn't deal with those qualities — music is concerned with sound, and painting or drawing with shape, isn't that so?

Hermogenes: Yes, certainly.

Socrates: Now, don't you think every single thing has its own essential nature, just like it has a color or shape? And even color and sound themselves, and anything else that really exists, each of them has its own nature, doesn't it?

Hermogenes: I think so.

Socrates: Well then, if someone could capture and imitate that inner nature of each thing through letters and syllables, wouldn't he actually show what each thing really is?

Hermogenes: Yes, definitely.

Socrates: So what would we call that person? You called the other imitators 'musician' and 'painter' — what about this person?

Hermogenes: I think he would be the name-maker we have been looking for all along.

Socrates: Exactly. So if that is the case, then the next thing to consider is whether, in the names you asked about — things like flow, movement, or restraint — the name-maker has, through letters and syllables, really managed to capture their true nature, or not.

Hermogenes: Of course.

Socrates: So let's see — are these really the only basic elements, or could there be others?

Hermogenes: I think there are probably more.

Socrates: Yes, that seems likely. So how do we divide them further, and where does the imitator even begin? Since the imitation of a thing's nature happens through letters and syllables, wouldn't it make sense to separate out the letters first, just like someone who wants to learn rhythm first studies the powers of individual sounds, then the syllables, and only then goes on to the patterns of rhythm?

Hermogenes: Yes, I agree.

Socrates: Then, I think we'd have to begin by dividing up the vowels, then within their types the consonants — which the experts sometimes call mutes — and also the letters that are neither pure vowels nor pure mutes, and then look at the kinds of vowels themselves, if there are classes among them, just as there are among letters in general.

And after we've made all those proper divisions, we should assign names to the things that deserve them, if there are names that can be linked back to those elements, and look at their nature, and whether they too have any kinds or classes, like the letters do.

When we've studied all that carefully, we would then know how to apply each letter to its proper place — sometimes using a single letter for a single thing, or combining several letters together. Just like painters, who sometimes use only one color, or sometimes many colors, to make an image of a statue or something else, choosing each color according to what the picture needs.

In the same way, we would apply letters to things — using a single letter when that fits, or combining many letters into syllables, and then combining syllables into nouns and verbs, and finally combining nouns and verbs into something great, beautiful, and complete.

Just as the painter made a full picture, we will build up language through the art of naming, or rhetoric, or whatever you want to call it. Actually, I spoke too quickly there — it wasn't really *us* who did this, but the ancients, who put language together the way it is now.

425a-426b: By Zeus! (Examining Scientifically)

And if we want to examine it scientifically, we have to take it apart again, just as they put it together, and see whether the names — both the early ones and the later ones — were formed systematically or not. Because if they were put together at random, then, my dear

Hermogenes, the whole thing is a rather poor and unscientific affair.

Hermogenes: By Zeus, Socrates, I think so.

Socrates: Well then — do you think you could actually take names apart in that kind of systematic way? I don't think I could.

Hermogenes: I'm sure I couldn't either.

Socrates: So what do you say? Should we give up? Or shall we do the best we can, and see whether we can understand at least a little bit about them? And just like earlier, when we said about the gods that we only had human opinions and no certain knowledge, let's also say to ourselves before we go further that whoever wants to investigate names properly will have to analyze them in that way — but for our part, let's do our best in every way we can. Does that sound good to you?

Hermogenes: Yes, I agree completely.

Socrates: It might sound ridiculous, Hermogenes, that things can be shown through imitation in letters and syllables — but there's no other option. There is no better principle for explaining the truth of the earliest names. Unless, of course, we want to take the easy way out, like the tragic poets who bring in gods on a crane whenever they get stuck. We could say, 'the gods gave the earliest names, so they must be correct.' Or maybe we could claim we got them from some foreigners who are older than us. Or that they're too old to discover, just like foreign words.

All those ideas are just clever ways of dodging the question for people who don't want to give a real explanation of what makes the earliest names correct. And you see, Hermogenes, if someone is ignorant about the correctness of the earliest names, he must also be ignorant about the later ones, because the later names are only explained by means of the earliest.

So it's clear that anyone who claims to have expert knowledge about names has to be able to give a clear explanation of the first names first — otherwise, what he says about later names will be nonsense. Don't you agree?

Hermogenes: No, Socrates, not in the least.

426b-427d: Socrates' Ideas About First Names

Socrates: Well then, my ideas about the very first names might sound pretty strange and even ridiculous, but I'll share them if you want — and if you can think of something better, please share it back with me.

Hermogenes: Don't be afraid, go ahead.

Socrates: First of all, I think the letter rho is a kind of tool for expressing every kind of motion. We haven't yet explained why the word *kinesis* means motion, but it really ought to be *iesis*, because the ancients didn't use the letter eta, only epsilon. And the root is *kiein*, which is a foreign word meaning the same as our *ienai*, 'to go'. So the old word would have been *iesis*, but after using this foreign *kiein*, then changing epsilon to eta, and adding a nu, it ended up becoming *kinesis*, even though maybe it should have been *kieinesis* or *eisis*. And *stasis* means standing still, the opposite of motion, but was made smoother for pronunciation.

So the name-giver, as I see it, thought the letter rho was a perfect instrument for representing motion, and used it a lot for that reason. For example, in words like *rein* (to flow), *roë* (current), *tromos* (tremble), *trechein* (to run), and in *krouein* (strike), *thrauein* (break), *ereikein* (tear), *thrupthein* (crush), *kermatizein* (crumble), *rumbein* (whirl) — in all these, the rho shows action, because the tongue moves the most and is least at rest when pronouncing that letter.

Iota, on the other hand, he used for all the fine, subtle things that pass through easily, so he imitated the nature of *ienai* (go) and *hiesthai* (hasten) with it. And phi, psi, sigma, and zeta he used to imitate things connected with breath or blowing, because these letters use a lot of breath when spoken — like in *psuchron* (cold), *zeon* (boiling), *seiesthai* (shaking), and *seismos* (shock).

He seems to have thought that the pressure of the tongue in pronouncing delta and tau was good for expressing binding and staying in place. And seeing how lambda lets the tongue slip, he used it for words like *leia* (smooth), *olisthanein* (slip), *liparon* (sleek), *kollodes* (sticky). When that slipping is stopped by a harder sound like gamma, it produced words like *glischron* (sticky), *gluku* (sweet), and *gloiodes* (gluey).

He noticed that nu is sounded from inside the mouth, so he put it in words meaning 'inside', like *endon* and *entos*. And he used alpha to show largeness, and eta to show length, because these letters are themselves big. Omicron he used for anything round, like *goggulon* (round), making it the key letter there.

In the same way, the name-giver seems to have chosen the rest of the letters, and from them put together the names for everything, and from those names he made all the others by combining and imitating.

That, Hermogenes, is what seems to me to be the theory of how names are correct — unless Cratylus has some other explanation.

Episode IV

426d-428e: By Zeus! (Cratylus Returns)

Hermogenes: Socrates, as I told you from the beginning, Cratylus confuses me terribly. He insists there is a *correctness* of names, but never makes clear what he means. I cannot tell if he speaks so cryptically on purpose, or just from habit.

Cratylus, with Socrates here listening, tell us plainly — do you agree with what Socrates has said about names? Or do you have a better account? If so, share it; then either you will learn from Socrates, or you will teach us both.

Cratylus: Hermogenes, surely you do not think that such a matter can be taught or learned all at once — especially one as serious as this, which seems to me among the very greatest and most demanding subjects of inquiry?

Hermogenes: No, by Zeus, I do not think it can be explained in a single moment. But I agree with Hesiod, that poet of moral and practical counsel, who says, "if you keep adding little to little, the work is worthwhile." So, Cratylus, if you can contribute even a small measure of understanding, do not hold back. You owe it to Socrates — and to me — to help us establish shared reason and the possibility of a common field of truth. Let us set each stone carefully into a strong wall.

Socrates: Cratylus, I do not claim certainty in these matters, nor do I stand firmly on any of the positions Hermogenes and I have explored together. These have been, for the moment, the best opinions I could shape in dialogue. So if you, Cratylus, have a view stronger than mine, do not hesitate to bring it forward. I will receive it willingly, as a fellow in the phalanx of logos and of shared reason. I will count myself as your pupil in the study of the correctness of names. And I would not be surprised at all if your understanding proved to be better than mine. For you have clearly given deep thought to these things, and perhaps have had good teachers to strengthen your ranks.

Cratylus: Yes, Socrates, I have indeed paid close attention to these matters, and perhaps I might even enroll you among my own students. Yet I suspect it is rather the other way around.

I am moved to speak to you as Achilles once spoke to Ajax in the embassy. As the Poet wrote: *"Ajax, descendant of Zeus, son of Telamon, chief among the people, All you have spoken pleases me and rests well upon my spirit."* So, Socrates, I think your words sound like oracles to me. I don't know if whether you have been inspired by Euthyphro, or whether some Muse has long dwelled within you unseen, helping you steer the rudder of logos toward the common field of truth.

Socrates: My excellent Cratylus, I have for some time been amazed at my own supposed wisdom, and I confess I cannot fully trust it. So I think it is best for us to test my words again. For there is no worse deception than deceiving oneself, when the deceiver is always present within, never departing even for a moment. That is a terrible companion to keep. Therefore, like the poet says, as good hoplites defending the possibility of shared reason and a common field of truth, we must avoid the blindness that provoked Achilles' wrath, and look "both forwards and backwards," so that we can steady the rudder of logos and keep our course true.

Let us then revisit what we have declared: that the correctness of a name is the power to reveal the nature of the thing named. Shall we hold this to be a satisfactory anchor for our ship of logos? Have we arrived at a shared reason and can now seek to establish a common field for truth?

428e-429b: Shared Reason

Cratylus: Yes, Socrates, I am fully persuaded by what you have said.

Socrates: So then, names are given for the sake of instruction?

Cratylus: Certainly.

Socrates: And that instruction is an art, with its own craftsmen?

Cratylus: Of course.

Socrates: And who are these craftsmen?

Cratylus: The lawgivers, as you said from the beginning.

Socrates: And does this art arise among men in the same way as the other arts? Let me clarify: among painters, some are better and others worse, correct?

Cratylus: Certainly.

Socrates: And the better painters produce more accurate paintings, while the worse produce poorer ones? And the same goes for builders—some build sound and beautiful houses, and others, less so?

Cratylus: That is true.

Socrates: Then should we also say that some lawgivers craft better names, while others worse?

Cratylus: No, Socrates — there I cannot agree with you.

Socrates: So you do not believe that some laws are better and others worse?

Cratylus: I do not.

Socrates: And so you must hold that no name is better or worse than another?

Cratylus: Yes, Socrates, I think that all names — so long as they are truly names — are equally correct.

429b-429e: Hermogenes' Name

Socrates: Well then, what shall we say about our friend Hermogenes and his name, which we mentioned earlier? Should we declare that it is not truly his name at all — unless he truly belongs to the lineage of Hermes? Or shall we say it is his name, but applied incorrectly?

Cratylus: Socrates, I would say it is not really his name at all. It merely appears to be his, but in truth belongs to someone whose nature actually matches the name.

Socrates: Then, if someone calls him Hermogenes, would that not be speaking falsely? Or perhaps it would not even be possible to say he is Hermogenes, if he is not?

Cratylus: What exactly do you mean, Socrates?

Socrates: Are you suggesting, Cratylus, that it is impossible to speak falsehood at all? For there have been, and still are, many people who do just that.

Cratylus: Socrates, I believe a man cannot say something which is *nothing*. For isn't that the same as trying to speak nothing? Surely falsehood is to say what is not — but how can what is not be spoken at all?

Socrates: Your reasoning is too subtle for a man of my age, my friend! But tell me this: do you think it is possible to *speak* a falsehood, even if not to *say* one?

Cratylus: No, Socrates, neither to speak it nor to say it.

Socrates: And do you mean he could neither utter it nor use it as a greeting? For instance, if someone met you as a guest, took your hand, and said, "Hail, Hermogenes of Athens, son of Smicrion" — would he be sending forth the right spear-point of logos, or would his aim fall wide, as though striking empty air?

Cratylus: I think, Socrates, that man would simply be producing hollow sounds, like hammering on a bronze pot, not directing his speech toward its proper mark.

429e-430c: Building a Ship of Logos

Socrates: Even that will do for my purpose. Tell me then — would those empty sounds be true, or false, or partly true and partly false? If we can agree on that, it will help us bore a straighter hole for the ship of logos, so its keel might hold firm.

Cratylus: I should say that the man's tongue would merely be set in motion for no reason, a clanging without measure or craft.

Socrates: Come then, Cratylus, let us look for a spot to drop our anchor for the ship of logos so we can create shared reason and the possibility of a common field of truth. Surely, you would grant that the name is one thing, and the thing named another?

Cratylus: Yes, I should agree to that, Socrates.

Socrates: And you would also say that a name is an imitation of the thing it names, as a kind of reflection?

Cratylus: Most certainly.

Socrates: And you would grant that paintings too are imitations, though they use a different art?

Cratylus: Yes.

Socrates: Then, let me test my understanding. Could both these imitations — paintings and names — be properly applied to the things they imitate, as if setting the rudder of logos toward its true course? Or not?

Cratylus: They could indeed.

Socrates: Let us look more closely. We can give the likeness of a man to a man, and of a woman to a woman, just as the shipwright fits each plank to its place?

Cratylus: Certainly.

Socrates: But we might also try, if we wished, to assign the likeness of a man to a woman, and of a woman to a man — steering the name off course?

Cratylus: That is possible.

Socrates: And would you say both of these are correct, or only the first?

Cratylus: Only the first.

Socrates: Then it is the assignment which places the likeness upon what truly belongs to it, as the spear-point of logos lands true, that is correct?

Cratylus: That is my view, Socrates.

430c-431c: Socrates Makes Declarations

Socrates: Then, dear Cratylus, since we are friends at sea together, let us steady the ship of logos and keep the phalanx in formation. Here is what I would declare.

I call the first kind of assignment — whether with paintings or names — correct, and in the case of names not only correct but *true*. This provides the ability to create a phalanx of logos and shared reason so that there is a possibility of a common field of truth.

But the other kind, which gives and applies what is unlike, I call incorrect. In the case of names, it is *false* and it steers the rudder of speech off its proper course so that there can be no shared reason and no possibility of a common field for truth.

Cratylus: That may be true for pictures, Socrates, that they might be wrongly assigned. But for names, I do not believe they can ever go astray — they must be always rightly guided.

Socrates: But what difference do you see, my friend? Can I not approach a man in the agora and say, "Here is your portrait," showing him either his true likeness or, perhaps, that of a woman — presenting it to the sight?

Cratylus: Yes, certainly.

Socrates: Well, can I not also stand before that same man and say, "Here is your name," since a name too is a kind of imitation? I might then bring before him the likeness of a man — or wrongly, the likeness of a woman — and say, "This is a man" or "This is a woman," though misnamed. Is that not possible, like a ship running aground when the helm fails?

Cratylus: I am willing to concede it, Socrates — you have kept the rudder of our ship of logos true. I agree.

Socrates: That is well granted, my friend, if I am steering correctly; then we can furl the sails of our dispute for the moment. If we allow, Cratylus, that names can sometimes be misapplied — that one might name the likeness of a man but mean a woman, or call a woman by the likeness of a man — then this same confusion of likeness and unlikeness holds. So let us say that when names are rightly applied, they stand firm in the phalanx of logos as *true*; but when they are wrongly assigned, they wander from their course and become *false*.

If that is so, then verbs also, Cratylus, can drift off course. And if verbs and nouns are subject to misnaming, then the entire ship of language — that is, the sentence, made of both verb and noun — may likewise founder. What say you?

Cratylus: I agree with you, Socrates; the rudder seems steady on that point.

431c-431e: By Zeus! (Identifying a Good Lawgiver)

Socrates: Now let us compare these first names to sketches — the earliest carvings on the prow of the ship of logos. These sketches might carry all the proper colors and shapes, or leave some missing, or even add strange excesses. And what if the likeness of a woman should appear with the helm of a man, or a man drawn with the braided locks of a woman? It would still be a picture, but not a faithful one.

Cratylus: Very true, Socrates.

Socrates: So then, just as the shipwright who shapes every plank true to its purpose fashions a seaworthy vessel, the one who sets down all the letters and syllables in proper measure makes a good likeness — a name that sails straight and steady. But if he leaves something out, or adds some timber that does not belong, the name remains a kind of sketch, yet it will list to one side like a ship poorly trimmed, or waver like a shield with a bent rim. In this way, some names are well-built, others poorly built. Is that not so?

Cratylus: I suppose it is, Socrates.

Socrates: Then just as one might call the shipwright or the spear-maker a good craftsman or a bad one, so too the maker of names, the lawgiver, must be reckoned good if he shapes them rightly — and bad if he shapes them poorly.

Cratylus: I grant it.

Socrates: By Zeus, then, if we stand by our earlier reasoning, it must follow that just as ships, shields, and spears may be made by better or worse artisans, so too the ship of logos, the whole lawgiving art of naming, may have its good and its poor helmsmen.

Episode V

431e-432d : Cratylus Controls the Rudder

Cratylus: That is how I see it, Socrates. You must admit, in the case of language, whenever by the craft of grammar we fit together the letters — alpha, beta, and all the rest — if one removes, or adds, or shifts even a single letter, then it is no longer truly a name at all. It becomes another thing altogether, a false plank in the ship, a broken spar on the mast, unfit for sailing.

Socrates: But let us pause, Cratylus. Perhaps you are steering us off course.

Cratylus: And why is that?

Socrates: I suspect, my friend, that you are thinking of those things whose very being depends on an exact count, as with numbers — where to add or subtract even a unit is to create a different sum. Ten ceases to be ten if you so much as scrape away a single one of its elements. But with images, or things defined by qualities, this strict accounting does not apply. If an image were forced to match its model in every respect — to capture each hidden grain, each secret joint of the keel, each breath of the soul — then it would cease to be a likeness at all. Imagine a divine shipwright who built not merely a likeness of your figure and your color, as painters do, but who forged in wood every internal fiber as well, gave it your same warmth, your same mind, your same living motion, until there was no difference left — what then? Would you say that this was a man named Cratylus and the ship of Cratylus? Or, are there now two Cratyluses built side by side?

Cratylus: I would say, Socrates, that there were two Cratyluses launched upon the sea.

Socrates: Then do you see, dear Cratylus, that we must search for a different standard of correctness, both for images and for names? We cannot demand that an image ceases to be an image simply because something has been added or taken away. Consider, my friend, how distant an image truly stands from the full nature of the thing it imitates, just as a model ship is distant from the sea-born vessel it portrays.

Cratylus: I see that, Socrates.

Socrates: And think how laughable it would be if names struck their target so perfectly that they became no different from the thing named. It would be as though a shipwright built a perfect twin of the ship of logos that was so exact that no one could tell which vessel was the true ship, and which the model. In that confusion, no captain could steer towards shared reason and no spear of logos could strike its mark to create a possibility of a common-field of truth.

Cratylus: That is quite true.

432d-433b: Socrates Makes a Demand

Socrates: Then let us not be faint-hearted, but rather steady our courage. Let us admit that one name may be well-crafted, and another ill-crafted. We must not demand that a name capture every detail of its thing, letter for letter, plank for plank, as if re-creating the entire ship. Instead, we must allow a name to sail close to the truth even with the wrong letter aboard.

And if one letter, as Hermogenes and I agreed when discussing the letters of the alphabet, then a whole word and, if a word, then even a clause or sentence may sometimes fail in detail. However, so long as it keeps the inner pattern of its meaning intact, it still names the thing truly. That is, words follow the logic of the letters of the alphabet.

Cratylus: Yes, I remember, Socrates.

Socrates: Very well, then. So long as the inner pattern — the timber holding our ship of logos together - maintains its meaning, then it still names the thing, even if the name does not carry all its proper letters. When it has all the proper letters, we can say it names well. When it has only a few proper letters, it names poorly.

Let us grant this name well and name poorly understanding, my friend. Otherwise, we shall end up, like the straying night-walkers on the roads of Aegina, losing our way and arriving too late.

If not these principles, Cratylus, you must find another principle of correctness in names. Don't simply admit that a name is a representation of a thing through syllables and letters. For if you maintain both, you will break our ship of logos and founder in the sea of contradiction.

Cratylus: Socrates, what you say seems reasonable, and I will accept it.

433b-433c: Socrates Suggests Going Further

Socrates: Then since we have agreed on this point, let us go further. If a name is to be rightly made, it must use the proper letters?

Cratylus: Yes.

Socrates: And the proper letters are those which are most like the thing named?

Cratylus: Certainly.

Socrates: So that is how a name, like a well-fitted plank in the ship of logos, is rightly set in place. But when a name is not well made, most of it may still carry true timbers, if it is to resemble the thing at all, though perhaps one crooked beam spoils the design. That is what makes it badly constructed. Do we hold this view?

433c-434b: Cratylus Begins to Concede

Cratylus: I suppose, Socrates, there is no use fighting you on this any longer, though it still troubles me to say that a name badly given is a name at all.

Socrates: But you do accept that a name is an imitation — a representation — of the thing?

Cratylus: Yes.

Socrates: And you agree that some names are primary timbers, while others are built upon them?

Cratylus: Yes, I do.

434b-435a: Returning to Hermogenes' Claim

Socrates: So then, Cratylus, if the first and primary names are to be true images of things, can you suggest any better method than shaping them, so far as possible, to match the nature of what they represent?

Or do you still prefer the account Hermogenes and many others offer — that names are like slave-names, mere conventions, serving only those who have agreed upon them beforehand, so that it would make no difference if the agreement called small "great" and great "small," so long as the community of speakers understood one another? Which path of steering do you choose?

Cratylus: Socrates, I hold that resemblance is immeasurably better than arbitrary signs.

Socrates: You speak well. In that case, if a name is to resemble what it names, then surely its letters — the elements from which it is built, the timbers of its design — must themselves be naturally fitted to resemble things, must they not? Think of it as a craftsman working with pigments: could he ever produce a painting true to life if there were no colors in nature that resembled what he wished to imitate?

Cratylus: That would be impossible.

Socrates: In the same way, we could never make names truly reflect their objects if the sounds — their building-block letters — did not have a nature somehow harmonized with the things they point toward. The letters are the first material of names, their planks and rudder, so to speak?

Cratylus: Yes, certainly.

Socrates: Then let us return to the question Hermogenes and I tested earlier. Would you agree that rho is the letter which best captures the sense of speed, motion, and a kind of harsh firmness? Or do you disagree?

Cratylus: I agree with you, Socrates.

Socrates: And you still agree, Cratylus, that lambda, as we discussed before, points toward softness, smoothness, and such gentle qualities?

Cratylus: Yes, Socrates, that seems right.

Socrates: Now, you know that what we call *sklerotēs* — "hardness" — is what the Eretrians call *skleroter*?

Cratylus: I do.

Socrates: Then tell me: do rho and sigma both carry likeness to the same quality, so that to them a final rho expresses what a final sigma does to us? Or do you think one of us uses the letter with no meaning at all?

Cratylus: No, Socrates, I think they mean the same, for both of us.

Socrates: But is that because the letters are alike in all respects, or only in some?

Cratylus: Insofar as they both suggest movement, they are alike, I would say.

Socrates: Then how about the lambda found in *sklerotēs*? Surely that lambda suggests something contrary to hardness — does it not call up a gentler feeling?

Cratylus: Perhaps, Socrates, it does not belong there at all. Like the names you analyzed with Hermogenes, perhaps a letter has slipped its mooring and needs to be corrected. I would not object, as you did before, to pulling out what is unsuited and setting a sturdier letter in its place — replacing the lambda with a rho, to steer the name's meaning more truly toward its proper harbor.

Socrates: Excellent, Cratylus. But tell me — when I say *skleron* with its ordinary pronunciation, do you not still understand what I mean?

Cratylus: I do, Socrates, but that happens through custom, not by nature.

Socrates: When you say "custom," do you mean anything different than "convention"? For what is convention but this: I launch a signal with a particular meaning, and you recognize that meaning? That is what you have in mind?

Cratylus: Yes, exactly.

Socrates: Then whenever I speak and you know my meaning, that is a kind of message sent and received — a sign passed from one pilot of logos to another?

Cratylus: Yes, Socrates, it is.

435a-436a: Socrates Explains His Position

Socrates: Then look, my friend: when I speak, the sign I give may come even from something unlike my intended meaning — as with the *lambda* in *sklerotes*, which is not exactly suited to express hardness. And if that is so, then you must have made a kind of compact with yourself, for it seems that both like and unlike letters, with the help of custom and agreement, serve to indicate. Even if you think custom differs from agreement, still we must say that it is *custom*, not only likeness, that directs our signaling, since it can show our meanings through both similarity and difference.

Since you do not object — I will take your silence for agreement — we may conclude that convention and custom each help steer our meaning safely across the sea of speech. Think, Cratylus, of numbers: how could you ever name each single number purely by likeness, unless you accepted convention as your anchor of correctness?

For my part, I still believe names ought, as far as possible, to resemble their referents; but this power of resemblance, as Hermogenes argued, seems too weak by itself and must be bolstered by the everyday tool of convention.

I suspect language reaches its best condition when its words, or as many as can be managed, are appropriate in likeness — and its worst when they are most remote from it.

But tell me now, what is the true function of names? What service do they really perform?

Cratylus: I believe, Socrates, that their function is to instruct — simply put, one who knows the names also knows the things named.

Socrates: I take it, Cratylus, that your meaning is this: that whoever grasps the nature of a name — given that the name's nature is in turn modeled on the nature of the thing — will thereby know the thing itself. For if name and thing stand as likenesses, then the science of one is the science of the other, since the same knowledge applies to things which are alike. Is that the idea you meant?

Cratylus: Yes, exactly, Socrates.

Socrates: Then let us weigh what sort of knowledge or instruction this amounts to. Do you suppose it is the best, or the only way, or do you think there might be another method alongside it, even if less complete? What is your view?

Cratylus: I maintain, Socrates, that this is both the best way and the only one.

Socrates: And do you also hold that someone who seeks to discover what is real — the truth itself — will discover it by these same means, through names alone? Or does this method belong chiefly to instruction, while inquiry and discovery might follow another course?

Cratylus: No, I stand by my claim that discovery as well as instruction should proceed by this same route.

436a-437a: The Stakes

Socrates: Very well — let us examine that together. Do you not see, Cratylus, that a person who tries to navigate reality by following names, tracking their meanings letter by letter, runs a serious risk of going astray? Like a pilot who steers only by the shapes of the sails, yet forgets the winds?

Cratylus: How so, Socrates?

Socrates: Well then, Cratylus, plainly the first name-giver, whoever he was, must have assigned names according to his own understanding of the nature of things — that is the argument so far, yes?

Cratylus: Yes, exactly.

Socrates: But if that understanding was mistaken, and he proceeded to fit names to it, what do you imagine happens to us, his heirs, who sail along after him in the same current? Would we not, one by one, fall into the same error?

Cratylus: But Socrates, surely that could not happen! The name-giver must have grasped the true nature, or else, as I have insisted all along, those words could never be names at all. And there is strong evidence for this: the names themselves are consistent among themselves.

Surely you have noticed, in all our discussion, how each name fits into the same pattern and points toward the same meaning?

Socrates: Yet that, dear Cratylus, is hardly an answer. For if the first builder of these names made a mistake at the very beginning, and then forced everything else to match that first mistaken plank, the rest of the framework would follow that same flaw, consistently — just as sometimes happens in geometry, where a tiny error in the starting line throws off the entire construction, though everything after appears harmonious. That is why, whenever we lay the keel of a great argument, we must look carefully at our first foundations. If they are true, all else will steer straight; but if not, the whole ship may run aground.

So I would be amazed, Cratylus, if names were truly consistent in their nature. Let us return to what we said before: that names seem to indicate to us that everything is in motion, in flux, carried by the current of becoming. Do you hold that this is what they signify?

Cratylus: Yes, Socrates — and I hold that they signify it correctly.

Episode VI

437a-437d: Revisiting the Best and Worst

Socrates: Let us revisit, then, the word *episteme* — knowledge — and see how ambiguous it is. It seems to suggest that it makes the soul *stand still* (*histēsin*) at things, rather than sail along with them, so that its opening syllables are better kept as we say them now, instead of replacing the *epsilon* with *iota*. Again, consider *bebaios* (firm, steadfast), which conveys stability and position, not motion. And look at *historia* (inquiry): it too suggests something that halts the flow, stops the current. Likewise *piston* (trustworthy) certainly signals a standstill, a barrier to movement.

Then think of *mneme* (memory), which plainly expresses *rest* within the soul, not the turning of motion. Yet on the other side, consider how *hamartia* (error) and *sumphora* (misfortune), if we go only by their forms, appear to resemble *sunesis* (intelligence) and *episteme* and all the other words carrying a good sense. Likewise *amathia* (ignorance) and *akolasia* (unrestraint) also look similar in form, since *amathia* could be heard as *poreia tou ama theo iontos* — "the journey of one going with God" — while *akolasia* might be read as *akolouthia tois pragmasin*, "keeping in step with the things themselves."

So even the words we usually take as worst seem suspiciously like those we regard as best. And, Cratylus, I am sure that if we took our time, we could uncover many other names that might make us doubt our judgment, and suspect that the name-giver intended not that things are in flux and motion, but that they remain at anchor, steady and unmoving.

Cratylus: Yes, Socrates, but you can see for yourself that the greater number of names still declare motion.

437d-438b: Are Names Controlled by the Demos?

Socrates: But tell me, Cratylus, are we to treat names like votes cast in an assembly, counting up their correctness by majority rule? Shall the true names be only those that happen to carry one particular meaning if more examples support it?

Cratylus: No, Socrates, that cannot be reasonable.

Socrates: I agree, my friend — not reasonable in the least. Let us then leave that question behind and steer back to the point from which we drifted. You will recall, a moment ago, that you said the first name-giver must have possessed knowledge of the things he named. Do you still stand by that?

Cratylus: Yes, I do.

Socrates: And you mean that the first name-givers, the very first to launch words into the world, knew the things to which they gave these names?

Cratylus: Yes, Socrates, they knew them.

Socrates: Then tell me this: by what names did they themselves learn or discover these things, if, as we agreed, there were no names yet in existence — and if we claim that knowing or discovering anything is impossible except by knowing the names?

Socrates: But how, Cratylus, could we claim that these first givers of names — these lawgivers — possessed knowledge, if there were no names yet set afloat, no language at all upon which to steer their inquiry? For if, as you argue, things can only be known by their names, how could they have known anything before naming had even begun?

438c-438e: Cratylus and First Name-Givers

Cratylus: Socrates, I believe the most truthful account is that the very first naming-power was beyond human — divine, in fact — and so those first names were necessarily correct.

Socrates: Then you think, Cratylus, that a god or spirit, giving names, would have let himself fall into self-contradiction? Or do you deny the argument we just shaped together?

Cratylus: Socrates, the names that belong to one of the two kinds we spoke of — I mean those that do not align with what is in motion — I do not believe they are truly names at all.

Socrates: Which group, dear friend? Those names pointing toward stillness, or those pointing toward motion? For surely we agreed just now that we cannot measure this question simply by counting numbers on either side.

Cratylus: No, Socrates, that would not be right.

Socrates: Then, Cratylus, since the names themselves are quarreling — some striving to steer us toward truth, others boldly claiming to *be* truth — by what compass shall we judge them? Surely we cannot trust other names to settle the dispute, since there are no further names beyond these. It is clear, then, that we must look for something beyond names, something that does not itself depend on them, to guide us toward which of these truly reveals the nature of things.

Cratylus: That seems to me the right course, Socrates.

438e-439a: Things Without Names

Socrates: Then if that is so, Cratylus, it would follow that things can, in fact, be discovered without names.

Cratylus: So it appears.

Socrates: Tell me then, by what other passage could we reach knowledge of things, except by the simplest and most natural way — through the things themselves, if they are kindred to one another, or through their own being? For what is alien and other than them would surely lead us not to them, but away from them, to something else.

Cratylus: That is a true course, Socrates.

439a-439d: By the Gods!

Socrates: But wait! By the gods, did we not earlier agree that rightly given names are like the things named, that they are their likenesses, their crafted images?

Cratylus: Yes, Socrates, we certainly did.

Socrates: Then if things can be learned either by way of names or by way of their own being, which route seems to you the truer and more seaworthy? Shall we try to learn first from the likeness — to discover whether it is a faithful and well-made likeness, and then from that to steer toward the truth it imitates? Or shall we set our rudder directly for the truth itself, and there discern both what is true and whether any likeness of it has been properly fashioned?

Cratylus: Surely, Socrates, it is better to sail straight for the truth itself.

Socrates: Indeed. But as to how a person might discover or reach such realities, that might be a question too deep for either of us to chart fully. Still, I think it is already a fine harbor we have reached, to see that one should pursue truth itself, and not set out in mere reliance on names — for it is far safer to travel through the thing itself than through the echoes and images of its name.

Cratylus: That is plain to me, Socrates.

439d-440a: One Last Name

Socrates: Then let us sound one further depth, lest we be swept away by the sheer force of many names pointing in the same direction. For suppose it should turn out that those name-givers, while believing all things were in motion and flux — which I myself suspect they did — were mistaken, and so whirled themselves and us into a kind of spinning eddy. Come, dear Cratylus, let us ask a question that often troubles my thoughts, like a dream at sea: shall we say there truly exists such a thing as absolute beauty, or absolute good, or any other absolute?

Cratylus: Yes, Socrates, I am convinced there is such a reality.

Socrates: Then let us consider the absolute itself — not whether this or that face, or any other such particular, is beautiful — and whether it is subject to flux or not. Would you agree that absolute beauty itself, at least, must always remain as it is?

Cratylus: That seems unshakable, Socrates.

Socrates: Then, Cratylus, let us consider: if it is true that things can be known either through names or through themselves, which way is better and surer? To learn from the image whether it is a good imitation, and to learn the truth it imitates? Or to learn from the truth itself, and from that see whether the image is rightly made?

Cratylus: Surely it is better to learn from the truth.

Socrates: Yes — though perhaps how to discover the truth is too great a question for us today, still it is worth agreeing that we must look to things themselves, not only to names, if we wish to anchor knowledge. Names may steer us, like a ship's rudder, but cannot hold us steady on their own.

Cratylus: That seems clear, Socrates.

Socrates: Let us not be too quickly convinced just because many names flow in the same direction, as if they were a current pulling our ship. For suppose the name-givers, believing that all things are in motion, forged their terms to match that belief — and yet the truth itself is not so. Would we not, like sailors following a false pilot, be swept into a whirlpool ourselves?

Cratylus: Yes, that is possible.

Socrates: Then tell me, my friend, do you hold there is an absolute Beauty, or Good, or any such reality that stands firm?

Cratylus: Yes, Socrates, I believe so.

Socrates: And is not the truly Beautiful always as it is, rather than being tossed about in constant flux?

Cratylus: It must be.

Socrates: Then let us ask: if something is always becoming something else, how could we ever say "it is" — how could we name it? For in the instant of speech it would already have shifted away. If it is ever the same, then at that moment it is not changing. And if it is always the same, it cannot change at all without losing its own form.

Cratylus: That seems inevitable.

Socrates: Nor can it be known. For as soon as the knower approaches, it has changed, and is no longer there to be grasped. There is no knowledge of what is in no stable state.

Cratylus: True, Socrates.

Socrates: Then, dear friend, let us conclude: the ship of logos may use names as its sail, but it must keep its keel set in the truth itself if it is ever to cross the open sea of being.

Exodus

440a-440d: Heraclitus (Socrates Questions)

Socrates: But, Cratylus, can there be knowledge at all if all things are in perpetual change, with nothing stable? If knowledge itself does not change, then knowledge would stand fast and exist. But if knowledge itself is always shifting, then whenever it changes, there would no longer be knowledge — and if change is unending, then knowledge, too, is lost. And so there would neither be anyone to know nor anything to be known.

Yet if there is that which knows and that which is known, if the beautiful, the good, and all other true realities exist, I do not see how these could resemble things in endless flux or motion. Whether the true nature of things is as we suppose, or as Heraclitus and many others claim, is a difficult question. But no reasonable person, I think, would place his mind under the tyranny of names, or trust completely in those who invent them, so far as to believe he has knowledge merely from words. Nor should a person condemn himself and all things around him to the disease of believing everything leaks and flows like broken pots, or that the whole world is like a man with a running nose.

Perhaps this doctrine is true — but perhaps not. Therefore, my dear Cratylus, you must reflect bravely and carefully, and not be too easily persuaded. You are young, strong, and in your prime; investigate with courage, and if you find the truth, come back and share it with me.

440d-440e: Heraclitus (Cratylus Embraces)

Cratylus: I shall do as you say, Socrates, though I assure you that after much toil and careful thought, I am still inclined to believe the doctrine of Heraclitus.

Socrates: Very well, my friend — another day, when you return, you shall teach me more; but for now, go on your journey to the countryside, as you planned, and Hermogenes will go a little way with you.

Cratylus: Agreed, Socrates. And I hope you will continue to steer your thought toward these matters as well.

www.ingramcontent.com/pod-product-compliance
Lightning Source LLC
Chambersburg PA
CBHW081641040426
42449CB00015B/3411